# 1 MONTH OF FREE READING

at

www.ForgottenBooks.com

By purchasing this book you are eligible for one month membership to ForgottenBooks.com, giving you unlimited access to our entire collection of over 1,000,000 titles via our web site and mobile apps.

To claim your free month visit: www.forgottenbooks.com/free911993

\* Offer is valid for 45 days from date of purchase. Terms and conditions apply.

ISBN 978-0-265-93367-1
PIBN 10911993

This book is a reproduction of an important historical work. Forgotten Books uses
state-of-the-art technology to digitally reconstruct the work, preserving the original format
whilst repairing imperfections present in the aged copy. In rare cases, an imperfection in
the original, such as a blemish or missing page, may be replicated in our edition. We do,
however, repair the vast majority of imperfections successfully; any imperfections that
remain are intentionally left to preserve the state of such historical works.

Forgotten Books is a registered trademark of FB &c Ltd.
Copyright © 2018 FB &c Ltd.
FB &c Ltd, Dalton House, 60 Windsor Avenue, London, SW19 2RR.
Company number 08720141. Registered in England and Wales.

For support please visit www.forgottenbooks.com

# FACTS AND SUGGESTIONS

### RELATIVE TO

# FINANCE AND CURRENCY

#### ADDRESSED TO THE

## PRESIDENT OF THE CONFEDERATE STATES.

### BY DUFF GREEN.

Anxious to promote the public interests as far as in my humble sphere I can do, I venture to suggest a plan for the restoration of the value of the public credit, which, I hope, if aided by your approval, will be adopted by Congress, and is therefore respectfully submitted for your consideration.

1. That all payments from the Treasury of the Confederate States be made in gold or else in coupon bonds, bearing a rate of interest which will be an equivalent for the use of money, or else in Treasury certificates bearing no interest, of denominations suitable for currency, not exceeding five hundred dollars, and convertible into bonds at the will of the holders.

2. That the bonds be of denominations not less than one thousand dollars, and convertible into certificates, deducting five per cent.

3. That all payments into the Treasury shall be made in gold or silver, or in Treasury Certificates.

4. That the Treasury Certificates shall bear date on the 1st of January, April, July and October, and, if not funded or paid on account of public dues, within six months from their date, shall be taxed five per cent., to be deducted when funded or paid; and if not funded or paid, as aforesaid,

comes necessary to increase the tax on the certificates, as a means of maintaining their relative value as money.

If, at a cost not exceeding the cost of Treasury Notes, I could, on the 1st of January, April, July and October, of each year, deposit in the Treasury of the Confederate Government and of each of the separate States, a sum, in gold, equal to the disbursements of each, for the next succeeding three months, no one would dispute my claim as a public benefactor. I propose to demonstrate:

1. That Congress have power to make the certificates thus to be issued a tender.
2. That the certificates, if made a tender, will be money.
3. That this *paper* money will be more valuable than gold as a circulating medium.
4. That this money will be more stable and uniform in value than gold.
5. That Congress can regulate the value of such a currency and cannot regulate the value of gold.
6. That the measures proposed would not only diminish the burden of the public debt, but would convert it into capital, which would be much more available and beneficial in the progress and development of our industry, our agriculture, our manufactures, and our commerce, foreign and domestic, than if the whole disbursements of our Government, State as well as Confederate, were paid in gold.
7. That under such a system of paper money, the States can organize a system of banking, requiring each bank to place ample funds with the Treasurer of the State for the redemption of their notes, to be held in trust, and applicable solely to that object.
8. That this would protect the public against loss by bank failures; and, at the same time, enable the banks to increase their line of discounts and to greatly increase their profits.
9. That whilst it would greatly increase the public and individual resources, it would greatly diminish the burden of taxation.
10. That such a reform in our system of finance would ensure the payment of the interest and principal of the public debt, in a medium of much greater value than that in which it was created.
11. That the conversion of our present system of currency into a metallic, or into a paper, convertible into a metallic currency, would inevitably cause so great a depreciation of the values of labor and of property, as to render the payment of the public debt impossible, and to make revo-

ake payment:

[. The measures which I propose will surely bring financial indepen-
, and prosperity, whilst the present system, if adhered to, will endan-
)ur political independence, and surely overwhelm us with national and
/idual bankruptcy, and with unexampled disgrace, distress and ruin
am aware that many believe that ours is a hard money Government
that nothing but gold or silver can be made a tender. I am also
e that many believe that it is impossible to prevent the depreciation
iper money. I am further aware that these opinions are so deeply
essed upon the public mind, that I must sustain my propositions by
ential and reliable authorities, as well as by argument.
proceed first to show what money is, and will then demonstrate that
ress has power to convert the Treasury Certificates into money, by
ng them a legal tender. The cause for which I plead, is the cause of
and Religious Liberty, of right, of justice, of good faith, of pecuniary
)endence, of human progress and prosperity; and I beseech you, the
ress, the Legislatures of the several States, and the people, for the
of that cause, earnestly to consider the facts and arguments which I
ctfully submit in support of it.            DUFF GREEN.

## WHAT IS MONEY?

orcester defines MONEY to be stamped metal, generally gold, silver
pper, used in traffic, or as the measure of price:—coin.

*EY differs from uncoined silver in that the quantity of silver in each piece of money
i'tained by the stamp it bears, which is a public voucher.—Locke.*
ash generally; any current token or representative of value, as bank notes ex-
3able for coin, notes of hand, accepted bills on mercantile houses, drafts, etc.
                                                                *Wright.*
—*Money*, originally stamped coin, is now applied to whatever serves as a circu-
medium, including bank notes and drafts, as well as metallic coins; *cash* is ready
, and is sometimes restricted to coin, or metallic money bearing a legal stamp;
is commonly used to include bank notes, drafts, etc.

Culloch, in his *Commercial Dictionary*, says:
en the division of labor was first introduced, commodities were directly bartered
ch other; those, for example, who had a surplus of corn and were in want of
endeavored to find out those who were in the opposite circumstances, or who had
lus of wine and wanted corn, and they exchanged the one for the other. It is
is, however, that the power of changing, and consequently of dividing employ-
must have been subjected to perpetual interruptions, so long as it was restricted
e barter. The extreme inconveniences attending such situations must early have
themselves on the attention of every one. Efforts would, in consequence, be
to avoid them, and it would speedily appear that the best, or rather the only
n which this could be effected, was to exchange either the whole or part of one
s produce for some commodity of known value and in general demand, and which,

consequently, few persons would be inclined to refuse to accept as an equivalent for whatever they had to dispose of. * * * * * *. *Now this commodity, whatever it may be, is money.*

An infinite variety of commodities have been used as *money* in different countries and periods. But none can be advantageously used as such unless it possesses several very peculiar qualities. The slightest reflection on the purpose to which it is applied must indeed be sufficient to convince every one, that it is indispensable, or at least exceedingly desirable, that the commodity selected to serve as *money* should be divisible into the smallest portions. 2d. That it will admit of being kept for an indefinite period, without deteriorating. 3d. That it should, by possessing great value in small bulk, be capable of being easily transported from place to place. 4th. That one piece of money, of a certain denomination, should always be equal in magnitude and quality to every other piece of money of the same denomination. 5th. That its value should be comparatively steady, or as little subject to variation as possible. Without the first of these qualities, or the capacity of being divided into portions of every different magnitude and value, *money*, it is evident, would be of almost no use, and could only be exchanged for the few commodities that might happen to be of the same value as its indivisible portions, or as whole multiples of them. Without the second, or, the capacity of being kept or hoarded without deteriorating, no one would choose to exchange commodities for money, except only when he expected to be able, speedily, to re-exchange that money for something else. Without the third, or facility of transportation, money could not be commercially used in transactions between places at considerable distance. Without the fourth, or perfect sameness, it would be extremely difficult to appreciate the value of different pieces of money; and without the fifth, or comparative steadiness of value, *money* could not serve as a standard, by which to measure the value of other commodities, and no one would be disposed to exchange the produce of his industry for an article that might shortly decline considerably in its power of purchasing.

The union of the different qualities of comparative steadiness of value, divisibility, durability, facility of transportation, and perfect sameness in the precious metals, doubtless formed the irresistible reason that has induced every civilized community to employ them as money.

John Taylor, Jr., defines *money* to be " a token issued by Government, and made a tender in payment of debts."

Adam Smith said :

A *paper money* consisting in bank notes, issued by a people of undoubted credit, payable upon demand, without condition, and in fact always readily paid as soon as presented, is, in every respect, equal in value to gold and silver money, since gold and silver money can at any time be had for it. *Whatever* is either bought or sold for such paper must necessarily be bought or sold as cheap as it could have been for gold and silver.

Ricardo says :

If there was perfect security that the power of issuing *paper money* would not be abused; that is, if there was perfect security for its being issued in such quantities as to preserve its value relatively to the mass of circulating commodities nearly uniform, the precious metals might be entirely discarded from circulation.

Mr. Calhoun, in his speech in the United States Senate upon the removal of the deposits on the 3d of January, 1834, said :

Whatever the Government receives and treats as money, is money in effect; and if it be money, they have the right under the Constitution to regulate it. * * * * *

If Congress has the right to receive anything else than specie in its dues, they have the right to regulate its value; and have a right, of course, to adopt all necessary and proper means, in the language of the Constitution, to effect its object.

McCulloch, under the title of "money," says :

No certain estimate can be formed of the quantity of *money* required to conduct the business of any country; this quantity being in all cases determined by the value of money itself, the service it has to perform, and the devices used for economizing its employment. Generally, however, it is very considerable, and when it consists wholly of gold and silver, it occasions a very heavy expense. There can, indeed, be no doubt that the wish to lessen this expense has been one of the chief causes that have led all civilized and commercial nations to fabricate a portion of their money of some less valuable material. Of the various substitutes resorted to for this purpose, *paper* is, in all respects, the most eligible. * * * * * Hence, the origin of bank notes.

These extracts not only prove that *money* may be made of *paper*, but that all civilized and commercial people have used paper money because it is more convenient and cheaper than specie; and that if not issued in excess, it is more valuable than specie.

In his speech upon the Sub-Treasury, Dec. 19th, 1837, Mr. Calhoun said:

"I am of the impression, to make this great measure successful, and secure it against reaction, some stable and safe medium of circulation, to take the place of bank notes, ought to be issued. I intend to propose nothing. It would be impossible, with so great weight of opposition, to pass any measure without the entire support of the Administration; and if it were possible, it ought not to be attempted where so much must depend on the mode of execution. The best measure that could be devised might fail and impose a heavy responsibility on its author, unless it met with the hearty approbation of those who are to execute it. I now intend merely to throw out suggestions, in order to excite the reflection of others on a subject so delicate and of so much importance—acting on the principle that it is the duty of all, in so great a juncture, to present their views without reserve.

It is then my impression, that in the present condition of the world, a paper currency in some form, if not necessary, is almost indispensable in financial and commercial operations of civilized and extensive communities. In many respects, it has a vast superiority over metallic currency, especially in great and extended transactions, by its greater cheapness, lightness, and the facility of determining the amount. The great desideratum is to ascertain what description of paper has the requisite qualities of being free from fluctuation in value and liability to abuse in the greatest perfection. I have shown, I trust, that the bank notes do not possess these requisites in a degree sufficiently high for this purpose.

I go further. It appears to me, after bestowing the best reflection I can give the subject, that no convertible paper—that is, no paper whose credit rests upon a promise to pay, is suitable for currency. It is the form of credit proper in private transactions, between man and man, but not for a standard of value, to perform exchanges generally which constitute the appropriate functions of money or currency. * * * * *

On what, then, ought a paper currency to rest? I would say, on demand and supply, simply, which regulates the value of everything else—the constant demand which the Government has on the community for its necessary supplies. A medium, resting on his demand, which simply obligates the Government to receive it in all of its dues, to the exclusion of everything else, except gold and silver—and which shall be optional with those who have demands on the Government to receive or not, would, it seems to me, be as little liable to abuse as the power of coining. It would contain within itself self-regulating power. It could only be issued to those who had claims on the Government, and to those only with their consent, and, of course, at or above par with gold and silver, which would be its habitual state; for, so far as the Government was concerned, it would be equal, in every respect, to gold and silver, and superior in many, particularly in regulating the distant exchanges of the country.

Nothing but experience can determine what amount and of what denominations might be safely issued; but it may be safely assumed that the country would absorb an amount greatly exceeding its annual income. Much of its exchanges, which amount to a vast sum, as well as its banking business, would revolve about it, and many millions would thus be left in circulation beyond the demands of the Government. It may throw some light on this subject to state that North Carolina, just after the Revolution, issued a large amount of paper, which was made receivable in dues to her. It was also made legal tender, but which, of course, was not obligatory after the adoption of the Federal Constitution. A large amount, say between four and five hundred thousand dollars, remained in circulation after that period, and continued to circulate for more than twenty years, at par with gold and silver during the whole time, with no other advantage than being received in the revenue of the State, which was much less than $100,000 per annum. I speak on the information of citizens of that State in whom I can rely.

Again, in a speech of Oct. 3, 1837, after demonstrating that in consequence of the receipt of bank notes by the Government they had in a great measure superseded the use of the precious metals, Mr. Calhoun said:

I am not the enemy, but the friend of credit. Not as a substitute, but the associate, and the assistant of the metals. In that capacity I hold credit to possess, in many respects, vast superiority over the metals themselves. I object to it in the form, which it has assumed in the banking system, for reasons which are neither light or few, and that neither have been or can be answered. The question is not whether credit can be dispensed with, but what is the best possible form—the most stable, least liable to abuse, and the most convenient and cheap. I threw out some ideas upon this most important subject in my opening remarks. I have heard nothing to change my opinion. I believe that Government credit, in the form I suggested, combines all the requisite qualities of a credit circulation in the highest degree, and, also, that the Government ought not to use any other credit but its own in its financial operations.

We are told that the form I suggested is but a repetition of the old Continental money—a ghost that is ever conjured up by all who wish to give the banks an exclusive monopoly of Government credit. The assertion is not true; there is not the least analogy between them. The one was a promise to pay when there was no revenue, and the other to receive in the dues of the Government when there was an abundant revenue.

We are told that there is no instance of a Government paper that did not depreciate. In reply, I affirm that there is none, assuming the form I propose, that ever did depreciate. Whenever a paper, receivable in the dues of Government, has anything like a fair trial, it has succeeded. Instance the case of North Carolina, referred to in my opening remarks. The drafts of the Treasury at this moment, with all their encumbrances, are nearly at par with gold and silver. I might add the instance alluded to by the distinguished Senator from Kentucky, in which he admits that as soon as the excess of the issue of the Commonwealth Bank of Kentucky were reduced to the proper point its notes rose to par. The case of Russia might also be mentioned. In 1827 she had a fixed paper circulation, in the form of Bank Notes, but which were inconvertible, of upwards of $120,000,000, estimated in the metallic ruble, and which had for years remained without fluctuation, having nothing to sustain it but that it was received in the dues of the Government, and that too with a revenue of only about $90,000,000 annually. I speak on the authority of a respectable traveller. Other instances might no doubt be added, but it needs no such support. How can a paper depreciate which the Government is bound to receive in all its payments, and while those to whom payments are to be made are under no obligation to receive it? From its nature it can only circulate when at par with gold and silver, and if it should depreciate none could be injured but the Government.

It will be seen that his purpose was to organize a financial system for the United States, in which the credit of the Government should be received and paid away at par with gold. Small as the minority in which he and his friends were, under the pressure of circumstances and the force of his arguments, Congress, in 1846, passed an act, which, as quoted by Colwell, provides " that the Treasurer of the United States, the Treasurer of the Mint of the United States, the Treasurers, and those acting as such at the various Branch Mints, all Collectors of Customs, all Surveyors of the Customs acting also as collectors, all Assistant Treasurers, all receivers of public money at the several land offices, all Postmasters, and all public officers of whatever character, be, and they are hereby required to keep safely, without loaning, using, depositing in banks, or exchanging for other funds than he is allowed by this act, all the public money collected by them, or otherwise, at any time, placed in their possession or custody, till the same is ordered by the proper department or officer of the Government to be transferred or paid out; that all collectors and receivers of public money of every character and description shall so frequently as they may be directed by the Secretary of the Treasury or the Postmaster General, to pay over to the Treasurers of their respective districts all public money collected by them, or in their hands; and it shall be the duty of the Secretary and the Postmaster General respectively, to order such payments by the said collectors and receivers at all said places, at least as often as once in each week, and as much more frequently in all cases as they in their discretion may think proper." It is farther enacted in the same statute, "That on and after the first of January, 1847, all sums payable to the United States shall be paid in gold or silver coin, or in Treasury Notes issued by authority of the United States, that on and after the first of April, 1847, all payments shall be made in gold or silver coin, or in Treasury Notes, if the creditor agrees to receive said notes in payment."

Colwell quotes from the Secretary of the Treasury's (Mr. Guthrie) report, of December 3d, 1855, as follows:

The Independent Treasury Act still continues eminently successful in all its operations. The transfers, for disbursements, during the fiscal year, to the amount of $39,407,674 03, have been made at a cost of $10,762 35, while the premium on the sale of drafts has amounted to $30,431.87. The receipts and expenditures during the fiscal year amounted to $131,413,859.59 have all been in the Constitutional currency of gold and silver without any perceptible effect upon the currency or upon the healthy business operations of the country.

And again from his annual report, December 1st, 1856:

The amount transferred, for disbursement, during the past fiscal year was $88,088,113 92, at a cost of $12,954.87; while the premiums paid on sale of Treasury drafts have been $54,924.16, leaving $41,978 29 over and above the expenses. The receipts and expenditures during the fiscal year, have amounted in the aggregate to $146,866,933,48, and have all been paid in the Constitutional currency of gold and silver without any disturbing effect upon the currency, the banks, or business of the country.

Commenting upon this act, Colwell says:

It proposed that all payments to and from the Treasury should be made in gold and silver coin, or in Treasury notes issued under the authority of the United States. Now this was offering to the creditors of the Government their choice of specie *or the very best currency which could be issued in the country*. No medium of payment which could be devised would better accommodate the public creditors than Treasury Notes, issued in forms and denominations to suit the wants and conveniences of the people.

I quote these extracts to demonstrate the correctness and wisdom of Mr. Calhoun's views of the proper use of public credit, intending, as I progress, to cite other facts, stronger if possible than these, to enforce the necessity of adopting the measures which I propose. It is true that the value of Treasury Notes, under the system adopted by the Federal Government, was kept at par with gold because the banks were required to redeem their notes with specie. I propose to make our Treasury Notes convertible into coupon bonds, worth as much as specie, and thus maintain their value.

## CAN CONGRESS MAKE TREASURY NOTES A TENDER?

In his speech upon the Sub-Treasury, delivered in the Senate March 10th, 1838, Mr. Calhoun said:

I do not deem it necessary to inquire whether, in conferring the power to coin money and regulate the value thereof, the Constitution intended to limit the power strictly coining money and regulating its value, or whether it intended to confer a more gene power over the currency; *nor do I intend to inquire whether the word coin is limited simp to metals, or may be extended to other substances, if through a gradual change they m become the medium of the general circulation of the world.* Whatever opinion there m be entertained in reference to them, we must all agree, as a fixed principle in our syste of thinking on Constitutional questions, that the power under consideration, like oth powers, is a trust power, and that, like all such powers, it must be so exercised as effect the object of the trust, as far as it may be practicable; nor can we disagree that t object of the power was to secure to these States a safe, uniform, and stable curren The nature of the power, the terms used to convey it, the history of the times, t necessity, with the creation of a common Government, of having a common and unifo circulating medium, and the power conferred to punish those who, by counterfeiting, m attempt to debase and degrade the coins of the country, all proclaim this to be t object. * * * * * * * *

*If Congress has a right to receive anything else than specie in its dues, they have a right to regulate its value, and have a right, of course, to adopt all necessary and prop means, in the language of the Constitution, to effect the object.*

Again, in reply to Mr. Webster, March 22d, 1838, Mr. Calhoun said:

I now undertake to affirm positively, and without the least fear that I can be answer —what heretofore I have but suggested—that a paper, issued by Government, with t simple promise to receive it in all its dues, leaving its creditors to take it or gold a silver, at their option, would, to the extent that it would circulate, form a perfect pap circulation, which could not be abused by the Government; that it would be as stea and uniform in value as the metals themselves; and that if, by possibility, it should preciate, the loss would fall, not on the people, but on the Government itself; for t only effect of depreciation would be virtually to reduce the taxes, to prevent which t interest of the Government would be a sufficient guarantee. I shall not go into t discussion now, on a suitable occasion I shall be able to make good every word have uttered. *I would be able to do more—to prove that it is within the Constitution power of Congress to use such a paper, in the management of its finances, according the most rigid rule of construing the Constitution;* and that those, at least, who thi that Congress can authorize the notes of State corporations to be received in the pub dues, are estopped from denying its right to receive its own paper. If it can virtua indorse by law, on the notes of specie paying banks, "Receivable in payment of t public dues," it surely can order the same words to be written on a blank piece of pap

As the power to coin "money" and regulate its value, and to pass laws necessary and proper to effect that object is expressly given Congress, and, as the purpose of the Constitution was to enable Congress give to the States "a safe, uniform, and stable currency," Mr. Calho refers to "the history of the times, and the necessity with the creation a common government of having a common circulating medium," support of his proposition, that whatever the Government may receive a pay away as money is money, and that it is the duty of Congress to regula its value.

What was the history of the times? and what was the necessity, creating a common and uniform circulating medium?

Ayres, in his *Financial Register* for 1857, in his chapter on Banks a Banking in the United States, says:

The first description of paper money, as far back as 1690, was in form of Bills Credit, secured on the property and revenues of the Colony, but war soon forced t

to increase this currency to such an extent, as greatly to depreciate its value
 with specie. This formed a very powerful difficulty with the States, yet it
 a legal tender, and received in payment of taxes and debts in New England
te of 6s. the Spanish dollar; in New York at 8s., and in Pennsylvania at 7s. 6d.
riations in the nominal value of the currency created the greatest confusion,
ay be understood by the difference between its nominal and real value in 1748,
ese bills, to the amount of $3,000,000, were issued. A bill on London for £100
 was equivalent to a bill for £1,100 of this paper money of New England; for
New York; for £190 of East Jersey; for £180 of West Jersey; for £180 of
ania; for £200 of Maryland; for £125 of Virginia; for £1,000 of North
; and for £700 of the paper currency of South Carolina. A part of these
ere soon afterward redeemed at two shillings in the pound, but the War of
dence, in 1775, called forth the increased demand for an extended currency.
in September of 1779, $160,000,000 were issued; when Congress passed a law
should never exceed $200,000,000, which sum it reached at the end of the
n 1780 and 1781 these bills ceased to have currency.

 was the "history of the times," which fully explains the necessity
ng to Congress, as the common agent of all the States, the exclusive
restricted power to coin money and regulate its value. The power is
coin *gold* and *silver* money. It is to coin *money*. This brings us to
iple question : What is money? And inasmuch as the unrestricted
 to coin money and regulate its value was given to Congress, without
ice to the material of which it is to be coined, the power to deter-
f what material it may be coined as well as the fineness, weight and
properties of money, is necessarily vested in the discretion of Con-
 For the clause forbidding the States to issue bills of credit, or to
anything else than gold and silver a legal tender proves that the proof our issue of paper money was under the consideration of the
ation which framed the Federal Constitution, and the fact that whilst
limited power to coin money and to regulate its value without
ice to gold, silver, or paper, was given to Congress, and the power to
aper money was not forbidden to Congress but was forbidden to the
is conclusive to prove that it was not the purpose of the Convention
id the issue of paper money by Congress.

t Mr. Calhoun would concur in this construction of the power of
ess, appears in the quotation given above. He said: "Nor do I
 to inquire whether the word coin is limited simply to metals, or
 extended to other substances, if through a gradual change they
ecome the medium of the general circulation of the world." There
 no other interpretation to this quotation than that, if under any
stances, it becomes necessary to issue paper money, then Congress
f they deem it expedient, *coin* paper money, and have power to pass
s necessary and proper to regulate the value of the paper money
oined, and consequently to make it a tender.

this view of the power of Congress, the Treasury Notes or Certifi-
ssued and paid away by authority of Congress, are money, and the
uestion is, is it necessary and proper to make them a legal tender as
ns of regulating their value? If so, then the power is vested in

## CONGRESS CANNOT REGULATE THE VALUE OF GOLD SO AS TO PREVENT FLUCTUATIONS IN THE QUANTITY AND VALUE OF A METALLIC CURRENCY.

The *Edinburgh Review*, of February, 1826, in a chapter on Banking says:

Let us then endeavor briefly to inquire into the circumstances that determine the quantity of money in a country; *first*, when the currency is wholly of gold or silver *second*, when it consists wholly of paper that is made a legal tender, but which is not convertible at pleasure into the precious metals; and *third*, when the currency consists partly of coin and partly of paper, immediately convertible into coin.

With respect to the first, or that in which the currency of any given country consists entirely of the precious metals, it is evident, inasmuch as they are always in demand and can be imported and exported at a very small expense, that the quantity of precious metals which such a country would, in all ordinary cases, use as money, would be limited to the quantity which was required to preserve their value at the same level in it, as in other countries. If, on the one hand, any greater additions were made to the amount of gold or silver in circulation, than were required to preserve the currency at this, its proper level, its value would fall, and there would, in consequence, be an *immediate exportation of the precious metals*; and if, on the other hand, the amount of gold or silver in circulation were unduly diminished, the opposite effects would be produced; the value of the currency would then be raised above its proper level, and there would be an importation of the precious metals from all the surrounding countries to restore that equality of value which could not in either case be permanently or even considerably deranged.

In the *second* case, we have supposed that of a country with a paper currency declared to be a legal tender, but not convertible at pleasure into the precious metals, it is evident, inasmuch as such a paper can neither be exported to other countries, when it is issued in excess, nor imported when the issues are unduly limited; that it is not possessed of the same principle of self-contraction and expansion inherent in a currency consisting of the precious metals; and that, consequently, its value must always depend on the extent to which it has been issued compared with the demand. * * * * *

The essential difference, then, between a currency consisting wholly of the precious metals and one consisting wholly of inconvertible paper, is this, that the value of the former, in any particular country, *can never differ, either permanently or considerably from its value in others; and that its value, as compared with commodities, depend on* the comparative cost of their and its production; whereas, the value of the latter, in any one country may vary to any conceivable extent from its value in others; and its value, as compared with commodities, does not depend on the cost of producing it and them, but to the extent to which it has been issued compared to the demand. * * * * *

It results from these principles, *that convertibility into gold and silver, at the pleasure of the holder, is not necessary to give value to paper money;* and that, if perfect security could be obtained that the power of issuing would not be abused, or that it would always be issued in such quantities as would render a one pound note uniformly equivalent to the quantity of standard gold bullion contained in a sovereign, the precious metals might be entirely dispensed with as a medium of barter, or used only to serve as small change. * * * * * * * *

We are naturally led to the consideration of the third and most important head in our inquiry, or to that which has for its object to discover the circumstances which determine the amount and value of the currency of a country when it consists partly of coin and partly of paper, immediately convertible into coin.

It appears, from what has been already stated, that an excessive quantity of the precious metals can never be imported into any country, which allows them to be freely sent abroad, *without occasioning their instant exportation*. But when the currency of any particular country, as of England, consists partly of the precious metals and partly of paper, convertible into them, the effects produced by an over issue of paper are the same as those resulting from an over issue of gold or silver. The excess of paper will not be indicated by a depreciation or fall in the value of paper, as compared with gold; but by *a depreciation of the value of the whole currency*, gold as well as paper, as *i that of other States.* \* \* \* \* \* It is obvious that this issue of ave precisely the same effect on the value of money as the issue of addigns. There cannot, it is clear, be any depreciation in the value of paper, as h gold; for gold may be immediately obtained in exchange for it, and it is given in all payments throughout the country. The effect of increased is, immediately convertible into gold, is not, therefore, to cause any discrein the value of paper and the value of gold, *in the home market,* but to amount of the currency, and by rendering it redundant or depreciated, *as h that of other countries, to depress the nominal exchange;* and thus, inqses do not circulate abroad, *to cause the exportation of coin,* and, *consein upon the bank.*

uoted thus at length from the *Review,* because it gives the argul upon by the advocates of a currency convertible into specie. gument of the Bank of England, and lies at the foundation of and of the measures and policy of that institution. It assumes, nasmuch as they are always in demand and can be imported and t a very small expense, the quantity of precious metals which ordinary cases, be used as money in any country in which the onsists entirely of gold and silver, would be limited to the quanmay be required to preserve their value at the same level in it countries. 2d. That the effect of a paper currency, convertible iu case of an over issue, will be to reduce the value of gold, as f the excess consisted of gold, and in like manner to cause an pecie. 3d. That the effect of a paper currency, which is a legal not convertible into specie, would be, that inasmuch as it would orted to other countries when it is issued in excess, nor imported ssues are unduly limited, its value may vary to any conceivable a its value in other countries; and its value, as compared with 's, does not depend upon the cost of producing it or them, but xtent to which it has been issued as compared with the demand. it results from these principles that convertibility into gold and ie pleasure of the holder, is not necessary to give value to paper l that, if perfect security could be obtained that the power of ild not be abused, or that it would always be issued in such as would render a one pound note uniformly equivalent to the standard gold bullion contained in a sovereign, the precious be entirely dispensed with as a medium of barter.

stitution authorizes Congress to " levy and collect taxes, duties, l excises for revenue necessary to pay the debts, provide for the fence, and carry on the Government of the Confederate States," 1oney and regulate the value thereof and of foreign coins," " To mmerce with foreign nations." " To raise and support armies."

States, then the power is expressly vested in Congress, and as Congress ha authorized the issue of paper money, it is the incumbent duty of Congres to make it a tender, because it is impossible otherwise to restore or main tain the value of Treasury Notes or Certificates as a circulating medium and, as Adam Smith, Ricardo, McCulloch, the *Edinburgh Review*, the *Lon don Quarterly*, Colwell, Mr. Calhoun, and all other reliable writers on th subject of currency, agree that if there is a perfect security that the powe of issuing paper money would not be abused—that is, that if there can b perfect security that it will be so limited in quantity as to maintain it value relatively to the value of the mass of circulating *commodities*—not c gold, but of the mass of circulating *commodities, nearly uniform*, then th precious metals may be entirely discarded from circulation.

It is this principle which gives value to the notes of non specie bank during their suspension—because, inasmuch as the public owe the bank more than the banks owe the public, and the debt due the banks must b paid in bank notes or in specie, the demand for bank notes for this us maintains their value as a medium of purchase as well as of payment; and they are received and circulated by the public because, although they ma not be a tender elsewhere, they are, a tender to the bank of issue, and a the sum in circulation is presumed not to be more than is wanted for pay ment to the banks, that fact gives them credit and currency. Now, I wil demonstrate not only that the Congress can, by a judicious system of fund ing and taxing, as I propose, so limit the quantity of certificates in circula tion, as to make them uniform and stable in value, as currency, but that inasmuch as they will not be subject to the contingencies which affect the value of gold in the foreign market, they will be more stable in value, and therefore a much better currency than gold.

The purpose of our Constitution was to enable Congress to create a com mon and uniform circulating medium for the people of the Confederate States If it be true, as asserted by the *Review*, and as I admit it to be that specie will be exported when the price in any foreign country is such as to pay a sufficient premium, and that it will return when the value be so much increased that the price in that country from which it was ex ported is so much greater than the price in that to which it was taken, as to pay a sufficient premium; then, as Congress cannot regulate the contin gencies which may affect the value of gold in any foreign country, and consequently cannot regulate the quantity or the value of specie in any other country, it is manifest that Congress cannot regulate the value of a metallic or of a paper currency convertible into specie. Inasmuch as Con gress cannot regulate the value of a metallic or of a paper currency con vertible into specie, and can regulate the value of a fundable paper issued by the Government, then as the exclusive power to coin money and to regu late its value is vested in Congress, it is the imperative duty of Congress to regulate the value of the paper money which they have authorized to be issued. The question is not whether Congress shall authorize the issue of paper money. It is, will Congress regulate the value of the paper money which they have already issued, and is its being a tender necessary to regu late its value ?

Can Congress discharge their duties in the exigencies in which we are ιced, without the use of the public credit, as money? If Congress is mpelled to use the public credit as money, who can deny the power of ngress to make it a tender, and to adopt all such measures as are necesry and proper to regulate its value? If we admit that the value of )ney, whether it be metallic or paper, depends upon the quantity in cir lation, and that it is a fixed law of a metallic and a convertible paper rrency that specie will be exported whenever its value is greater in any reign market, and that it is a fixed law of paper currency not convertible to gold, that if the quantity in circulation be no more than is requisite r use as money, it will be of equal value as gold, and that the precious etals in such case may be dispensed with, then it follows that if Congress akes the paper, which they issue, a tender, and reduces the quantity in rculation to the sum required for use as money, the paper thus issued ay be made as stable and uniform in value as gold. Can Congress, by a idicious system of taxing, cause the excess of their issues to be funded? f five per cent. tax will not suffice, then impose a tax of ten per cent., but ιy earnest belief is that the tax proposed will be sufficient.

As such a currency will not be subject to the general laws which reguιte the quantity and value of specie, it will be more uniform and stable in alue than gold. For it is admitted that if, from any cause, gold is more aluable in England than elsewhere, then the quantity of gold in England ιll be so increased by importation from abroad, that its value will be reuced to the same level as it may be in the foreign countries from which t may have been imported; then, if it shall appear that the importation f gold will necessarily continue long after the requisite supply of specie ιas been obtained, and that the inevitable consequence will be an undue xpansion of the currency to be followed by a re exportation of specie, and, onsequently, by an undue contraction of the currency, then it follows that he precious metals, being thus liable to be increased and diminished in [uantity, must necessarily fluctuate so much in value that it is impossible o predicate upon them a stable and uniform currency. This truth is orcibly illustrated by the annexed table, prepared with great care from uthentic official sources :

*Table showing the rate of interest charged by the Bank of England at the dates given, the quantity of bullion in the Bank, the notes in circulation and the notes in reserve, with a statement of the loans of the Banks of the City of New York, the amount of their notes in circulation, and of the specie in their vaults, given in millions, omitting the small fractions.*

| DATE | BANK OF ENGLAND ||||  Banks in the City of New York |||
|---|---|---|---|---|---|---|---|
|  | Rate of Interest per cent. | Bullion in Millions | Notes in Circulation in Millions | Notes in Reserve | Loans in Millions | Specie in Millions | Circulation in Millions |
| 1852. Jan. 1 | $2½ | $88 | $96 | $58½ | $ ... | $... | $... |
| April 22 | 2 | 98 | 106 | 57¼ | ... | ... | ... |
| 1853. Jan. 6 | 2½ | 99 | 117 | 49 | ... | ... | ... |
| Jan. 20 | 3 | 97 | 118 | 42¼ | ... | ... | ... |
| June 2 | 3½ | 91 | 117 | 41½ | ... | ... | ... |
| Sept. 1 | 4 | 82 | 112 | 38½ | 92 | 11 | 9½ |
| Sept. 15 | 4½ | 79 | 112 | 34½ | 90 | 11¾ | 9½ |
| Sept. 29 | 5 | 78 | 113 | 31 | 90 | 11¼ | 9½ |
| 1854. May 11 | 5½ | 63 | 105 | 23½ | 90¾ | 11½ | 9¾ |
| Aug. 3 | 5 | 66 | 101 | 31 | 93¼ | ... | ... |
| 1855. April 1 | 4½ | 75 | 96 | 42½ | 94½ | 15 | 7¾ |
| May 3 | 4 | 78 | 100 | 53½ | 93 | 14⅓ | 8 |
| June 14 | 3½ | 90 | 97 | 59½ | 93 | 15 | 7½ |
| Sept. 6 | 4 | 71 | 101 | 37½ | 100 | 12 | 7¾ |
| Sept. 15 | 4½ | 68 | 98 | 37½ | 99 | 12¼ | 7½ |
| Sept. 27 | 5 | 64 | 101 | 31 | 97½ | 10 | 7¾ |
| Oct. 4 | 5½ | 60 | 101 | 32½ | 95½ | 11 | 7¾ |
| Oct. 18 | 6–7 | 55 | 102 | 31½ | 95 | 12½ | 7¾ |
| 1856. May 22 | 6 | 51 | 96 | 49½ | 102¼ | 13¾ | 8⅓ |
| May 29 | 5 | 56 | 98 | 51 | 102½ | 14 | 8¼ |
| June 26 | 4½ | 65 | 98 | 62 | 107 | 17 | 8¼ |
| Oct. 17 | 5 | 54 | 105 | 51 | 105 | 10¾ | 8½ |
| Oct. 26 | 6–7 | 51 | 103 | 47½ | 104 | 10½ | 8½ |
| Nov. 13 | 7 | 48 | 99 | 45 | 103½ | 12¼ | 8¾ |
| Dec. 4 | 6½ | 52 | 96 | 49½ | 106¾ | 12¼ | 8¼ |
| Dec. 18 | 6 | 53 | 93 | 49½ | 108¼ | 11 | 8¼ |
| 1857. Jan. 1 | 6½ | 45 | ... | ... | 109 | 11 | 8¼ |
| June 1 | ... | 55 | ... | ... | 115⅓ | 13 | 8¾ |
| Sept. 1 | 5 | 57 | ... | ... | 112¼ | 10¼ | 8½ |
| Oct. 1 | 6½ | 50 | ... | ... | 106 | 11½ | 8 |
| Oct. 20 | 7 | 47 | ... | ... | 97¼ | 7¾ | 8 |
| Oct. 30 | 8 | 45 | ... | ... | 95 | 12¾ | 6¾ |
| Nov. 15 | 9 | 40 | ... | ... | 96½ | 16½ | 6½ |
| Dec. 10 | 10 | 35 | ... | ... | 96½ | 26 | 6½ |
| Dec. 21 | ... | 45 | ... | ... | 97¼ | 28 | 6½ |
| Dec. 31 | ... | 50 | ... | ... | 98 | 27½ | 6½ |
| 1858. Jan. 1 | ... | 60 | ... | ... | 98½ | 28½ | 6½ |
| March 1 | ... | 85 | ... | ... | 105 | 32¾ | 6¾ |
| Aug. 1 | ... | 80 | ... | ... | 120¾ | 35½ | 7¾ |
| Oct. 1 | ... | 95 | ... | ... | ... | ... | ... |

t will be seen that the average of specie and bullion hel England, from January 1, 1852, to October 1, 1858, w: e millions of dollars. If we assume this to be the "*pro* fluctuations between ninety.nine and thirty five millions various fluctuations between *two* per cent. and ten per c interest, as charged by the Bank, show that specie, as a Bank of England, instead of being the basis of a stab rency, is no more than the medium, through the agency nied men are enabled, by the use of their credit and the Exchanges, to control and regulate not only the value values of property—spreading ruin and bankruptcy bros the world, enriching themselves by creating those fluc ues of money and of property; which, as they declare, it prevent.

It should be remembered that it was the wars in India a ated an extraordinary demand for specie in 1857. That ncement of the war in the Crimea to the close of the wa ina, the export of specie from the United States was ndred and eighty millions of dollars. That the averag lks of the city of New York, from 1st July, 1852, to th 57, was $11,774,785; and that Gibbon, in his history o suspension in New York in 1857, says that although tl llions of dollars withdrawn between the 10th and 17th pletion in coin was but $5,483,864; and yet he says that 1 nic, created by the loss of this sum in specie, was that count of bills by the banks had mostly been suspendec es for money, even on unquestionable securities; rose to n five per cent. a month. *On the ordinary securities of promissory notes and Bills of Exchange, money was not e.* House after house, of high commercial repute, su nic, and several heavy banking firms were added to the *  *  *  *   Commercial business was suspen e avalanche of discredit swept down merchants, banker ions and manufacturing companies, without distinction cumulated capital, which had withstood the violence of a re prostrated in a day, and when they believed themselve fe against misfortune."

He gives a list of the sales at the broker's board of b nich, he says, includes a wide range of securities, from at are called "fancy," which shows an average depr an one-third. These securities represented a class of inv vertible into bonds bearing six per cent. interest, and reconvertible into certificates which were a legal tender, and the banks had held twelve millions of such bonds, instead of twelve millions of specie, there would have been no panic—there would have been no run for specie—no failure of merchants, bankers, monied corporations, and manufacturing companies—there would have been no depreciation of the value of bonds and stocks, and no loss of hundreds and hundreds of millions of dollars in the exchangeable values of property.

Is it not apparent that a system of paper money, made a legal tender, resting upon the public credit as a basis, and *regulated* by a judicious system of funding and taxation, may be made more stable and uniform in value than the system of banking and currency as *regula'ed* by the Bank of England? And this, I affirm, is the question involving no less our interests and welfare than the question of our political independence. We have no alternative—we must adopt a system of finance which can be regulated by our Congress, or the values of our credit, of our currency, and of our property, will be regulated by the Bank of England, and the combination of monied men of whom that bank is but the agent.

In June, 1852, the Bank of England held more than one hundred millions of dollars of bullion and specie, and interest was but 2 per cent, and that on the 10th of December, 1857, this sum was reduced to thirty-five millions, and the bank interest was *ten per cent.*—the effect of this pressure, on the London market, was that by the 1st of October, 1858, the bullion and specie in the bank had again increased to ninety five millions, and the rate of interest was again reduced.

The power of the Bank of England over the currency and credit of all foreign commercial nations is forcibly exhibited by the ruinous effect upon the credit and currency of the city of New York, and the consequent value of property. The average of specie held by the Banks of the city of New York, from 1st September, 1853, to 20th October, 1857, was, say eleven and a half millions of dollars; the pressure by the screw of the Bank of England reduced this quantity to $7,843,231, and interest rose to "three, four and five per cent. a month,". "on unquestionable securities," and the exchangeable value of property depreciated one third. But the table before us shows that, although the demand for specie in London to meet the disbursements of the wars in the Crimea, and in India and China, had reduced the bullion and specie in the Bank of England from ninety nine millions, in June, 1853, to thirty five millions in December, 1857, and had reduced the specie in the Banks of New York from seventeen millions, on the 26th of June, 1856, to $7,843,231 on the 20th October, 1857, yet the effect of the pressure by the Bank of England, and of the refusal of the Banks of New York to discount the best commercial paper, was to cause such a movement of specie that, whilst the bullion in the Bank of England had, on the 1st of October, 1858, increased from thirty five millions to ninety five millions, the specie in the Banks of New York had, on the 8th of May, 1858, increased from $7,842,231 to $35,453,146.

Does it require argument to prove that this fluctuation in the quantity of specie held by the Bank of England and the banks of New York, and in he rates of interest charged in London and in New York, was the consequence of the fact that the currency in London and New York was a convertible paper, predicated on a specie basis, and that, by refusing to renew discounted commercial paper and increasing the rate of interest, the demand for specie caused it to flow toward London and New York, the controlling commercial centres, until the accumulation was much beyond the sums requisite to maintain the value of specie at the *"proper level?"* Thus we see that the average held by the Bank of England was sixty-three millions, and that the average of the banks of New York was a fraction more than eleven millions, yet as soon as the banks in London and New York applied the screw with sufficient force, the quantity in the Bank in London rose from thirty-five to ninety-five millions, and the sum in the banks of New York rose from less than eight to more than thirty five millions. Thus, the tide rose in London more than fifty per cent., and in New York to more than three hundred per cent. above the "proper level;" and it is worthy of note that the fluctuation of the quantity of bank notes, in London and New York, was much less under this severe pressure of the bank screw than the fluctuation of the quantity of specie. Thus the diminution of specie in the Bank of England was sixty four millions, whilst the reduction of bank notes was but twenty five millions, and the loss of specie by the New York banks under the panic was $5,483,864, whilst the notes in circulation were reduced but one million and a half.

Is it not apparent, from these facts, that, if the value of money is regulated by its quantity, the fluctuations in the quantity of specie being greater than the fluctuations in the quantity of bank notes, a paper currency, made legal tender and predicated on an issue of public credit, and regulated by a proper system of funding and taxation, will be more stable and uniform in value than it is possible for a metallic or convertible paper to be? Is it not apparent that, if from any cause, gold is so much more valuable in London than it may be in the foreign market, that the Bank of England finds it necessary to so increase the rate of interest, and so reduce the discounted commercial paper as to cause the precious metals to flow back to London, the same pressure of the Bank screw which forces gold to flow from New York to London, will cause it to flow from South America, from Africa, from India and China, and from the Mediterranean and Continental Europe to London? And if we assume that sixty three millions in the Bank of England indicates the proper specie level for England, and that eleven and a half millions in the Banks of the city of New York indicates the proper specie level for the United States, is not the fact that immediately after the pressure by the Bank of England, in December, 1857, the specie in that Bank increased from thirty-five millions to ninety-five millions, and that it also increased in the Banks of the city of New York from less than eight millions to more than *thirty-five* millions, conclusive to prove that Congress cannot regulate the quantity or the value of the precious metals; and that the public credit, in the form which I propose, may be so regulated as to create a currency more uniform and stable in value than gold? The purpose of the Constitution is to establish justice, insure domestic tranquility, and secure the blessings of liberty to ourselves and our posterity.

2

Is it just that we should be compelled to pay a debt in a currency worth, to the creditors, twenty times the sum which they paid for it? Take the case of those who have made fabulous millions by dealing in foreign merchandise purchased with the public credit at the rate of twenty dollars of Treasury Notes for one of gold. Is it just that we shall be compelled to pay them one hundred and twenty per cent. per annum interest, when our promise is to pay them but six per cent.? And will not the payment, in gold, of six per cent. interest on the nominal amount of the debt, be equivalent to the payment of one hundred and twenty per cent. on the debt created? If the interest is paid in a currency of equal value to that in which the debt was created, will not the just claims of the public creditor be discharged? If, instead of making payment in the same medium in which the public debt was contracted, we are compelled to pay it in a medium worth twenty times as much, will we not increase the public debt twenty fold, and will not this increase the burden of the debt more than one hundred fold? Mr. Calhoun estimates the relative value of the property, as compared to the money of a commercial country, to be thirty for one. If we assume the amount of our public debt to be only two thousand millions of dollars, contracted in a medium so depreciated that it requires twenty paper dollars to purchase one of gold, the effect, upon the values of property, of paying that debt in gold will be not as twenty to one, but as thirty times twenty to one—that is, not only to increase the *burden* of our debt, payable in the medium in which it was created, to forty thousand millions of dollars, but to thirty times forty thousand millions of dollars—for whilst it will increase the value of the medium of payment twenty fold, it will reduce the value of our property thirty fold, and thus it will consequently increase the *burden* of debt and taxation in the same relative proportions, for the burden of the debt will be increased in the same proportion as the exchangeable value of our labor and of our property is diminished. If, on the other hand, we make payment in the same medium in which the debt was contracted, and so regulate that medium as to increase its exchangeable value nearly or quite twenty fold, and thus maintain the exchangeable value of our property, and at the same time that we diminish the burden of the public debt, relatively increase its value in the hands of the public creditor, the hopes of calculating avarice may be disappointed, but who can deny that the fullest claims of justice will be satisfied?

But, under the Constitution, Congress have power to regulate "commerce with foreign nations," and under that power can transfer to England, and to those who consume British goods, a large part of the burden of our public debt. As we progress, it will be seen that England is chiefly responsible for the war in which we are now engaged, and that strict justice, as well as a wise political economy, calls for the measures of retaliation which it is in our power to inflict.

In the Cotton Planters' Convention, held in Macon on the 4th July, 1861, I suggested the propriety of the purchase, by the Confederate Government, of the entire Cotton crop, as a means of sustaining the credit of the Government and providing funds for prosecuting the war. It was in reply to my personal argument, urging the propriety and necessity of this measure, that Mr. Memminger issued his remarkable letter, intended to act on the business convention held in Macon, in October, 1861, in which he denied the power of Congress to authorize the purchase of Cotton!! There are none, now, so blind as not to see the propriety of my suggestion, and the culpable ignorance, to call it by no harsher name, of the Secretary of the Treasury. Cotton is now worth, in Liverpool, from fifty six to sixty cents per pound. The present high price is the result of a deficient supply, and the impossibility of obtaining it elsewhere than from the Confederate States. If the market is thrown open, the competition will soon reduce the price to less than one third the sum which the Government could realise if Congress were to authorize the purchase and hold it for an arbitrary price. The monopoly of tobacco by France and the high duties levied by England illustrates the effect. If we assume that the average cotton crops for the next ten years after peace will be but four millions of bales, of five hundred pounds each, and the whole is purchased at a price which will enable the Government to pay the producers twice the sum which they could otherwise obtain, and yet leave a margin of profit as great or greater than the price paid the producers, it is obvious that the monopoly by the Government would not only greatly benefit the producer, but place in the public Treasury ample specie funds to sustain the public credit so as to render the Treasury Certificates equal to gold. Say that the Government price to the producer was fixed at thirty cents per pound, and to the consumer at sixty; this, upon the four millions of bales, would give six hundred millions of dollars per annum to the producers and a like sum to the Government. If to this be added the like profits on our tobacco and naval stores, it will be seen that a wise administration of our finances will enable us to pay our public debt and maintain the value of our currency. If the producer is unwilling to sell, and prefers a foreign market, then let the export duty be such as to protect the value of that purchased by the Government, and secure the profits on the Government monopoly.

---

CAN CONGRESS MAKE TREASURY CERTIFICATES A TENDER?

I am aware that it is believed by some that Congress cannot make Treasury Certificates a legal tender, alleging that the effect will be to impair the obligation of contracts. The Federal Constitution provides that Congress shall pass no law impairing the obligation of contracts, and yet under the power to enact a bankrupt law, the old Congress released bankrupt debtors from the obligation to pay their debts. Our Constitution provides that "no law of Congress shall *discharge* any debt contracted before the passage of the same." To authorize payments in the certificates which Congress have issued and paid out as money, will not be to discharge the debt without payment. As properly remarked by Mr. Calhoun, the meaning and purpose of the Constitution are explained by reference to the history of the times and the circumstances connected with its adoption. Ours, with the exception of a few modifications, is a transcript of the Federal Constitution—that part which gives to Congress power to coin money and to regulate its value is a literal copy. We, therefore, recur to the purpose of granting these powers, and find that it was "to secure to the *States* a safe, uniform and stable currency," and that it was given to Congress, because, if each State were permitted to coin money and regulate its value, and to make the money coined by them a legal tender, there would be no guarantee that each would not coin money for itself, and that, instead of having a money common to all the States, and of equal value in all, the value of the money of the several States would not be as various as the coinage and regulations of each might vary from the coinage and regulations of the other States. Thus the money of account of England is pounds and shillings; of France, livres and francs; of Germany, the Rix dollar; of Russia, the ruble, and of Spain, the dollar. As all contracts are made, and books and accounts are kept in the money of account, the necessity of having, for a people living under a common government, one common money of account, is obvious; and hence the necessity of vesting the power of coinage and regulating the value of money in Congress. If an Englishman, a Frenchman, a German, an American, and a Russian, were each, in his own money of account, to offer to purchase the same property, one offering to pay in sovereigns, another in livres, another in Rix dollars, another in rubles, and the other in American dollars, scarce one man in a million could estimate the relative value of the several offers, because all men are accustomed to the money of account of that country in which they live, and in which their transactions are made, and few, very few are sufficiently familiar with the money of account of other countries to use it in the purchase or sale of commodities without an estimate of its value in their own money of account. Thus, as the Spanish dollar was current in the States, and was worth in the money of account of New York eight shillings, whilst it was worth in the money of account of Virginia but six, if a citizen of New York were to offer thirty shillings per barrel for flour, the Virginian would inquire what shilling was meant? the shilling of New York or of Virginia? Was the offer at the rate of eight or six shillings to the dollar? As I have before remarked, it was not the purpose of our Constitution to restrict our Congress to the coinage of *gold* or *silver*. It was not to prevent the use of paper money, for inasmuch as it did forbid the States, and did not forbid Congress, to make paper money a legal tender, and gave to Congress an unlimited control over the coinage and the value of money, it is conclusively apparent that the subject of paper money was under the consideration of the Convention, and that Congress may, in their discretion, coin paper money. To me, it is an unanswerable argument in favor of the exercise of this power by Congress, that the purpose of the Constitution being to create, for the people of the Confederate States, a safe, uniform and stable currency, Congress can so regulate the value of paper money not convertible into specie, as to make it safe, uniform and stable in value, and cannot so regulate the value of a metallic or of a paper currency convertible into specie. It is generally assumed and admitted that the value of the precious metals, as well as of paper money, depends upon the quantity in circulation. I hold that this principle is modified by the circumstances under which they are used, and that their value, and the quantity requisite to maintain their relative value as compared with other commodities, depends upon the regulations which control domestic and foreign commerce.

Experience fully proves that the value, in the foreign market, of cotton, rice, sugar, naval stores and tobacco, does not depend upon the cost of production in the home market, but that it does depend upon the circumstances under which they are sold in the foreign market.

We have seen that the Constitution took from the States the power to coin money and regulate its value, and gave it to Congress because the purpose was to create a common currency, of uniform value in all the States, and experience had proved that it was necessary to deprive the States of the power to coin money and to regulate its value, and vest it in Congress as the common agent of all the States, as the only means of preventing that confusion and diversity of the money of account and depreciation of the value of the currency, which had been the result of the control over the coinage and the currency theretofore vested in each of the several States. We have also seen that the power which the Bank of England can exert over the currency of all other countries, which is predicated on a specie basis, is such, that, by refusing to renew the discount of commercial paper, and increasing the value of money in London, by increasing the rate of interest, that bank can compel the banks in the United States to suspend specie payments, as was the case in 1857, when but for the demand in London for specie to pay the expenditures of the wars in the Crimea, and in India and China, there would have been no pressure upon our banks, and no depreciation in the exchangeable values of our property; whereas, the actual depreciation was from thirty to fifty per cent. or more. Is it wise, or can any one believe that it was the purpose of the Constitution to vest in the Bank of England that power over our currency of which it was the purpose to deprive the States? What is the Bank of England, and what are the motives, and who are the persons, and what are the interests that regulate its measures and policy, that we should give to that Bank a control over the values of our currency, and of our credit and property, of which we have deprived the Legislatures of our own several States? Are not the directors and managers of that Bank English merchants, whose duty it is to exert the powers and influence which they possess for the advancement of British interests?

### THE BANK OF ENGLAND.

It is proper that, at this point, we should pause and inquire, WHAT HAVE BEEN THE MOTIVES WHICH HAVE REGULATED THE MEASURES AND POLICY OF THE BANK OF ENGLAND? And what has been the effect of the financial management of that Bank? It originated in a loan at eight per cent. of six millions of dollars to the Government, and became the agent of the Government in the collection and disbursement of the public revenue. Besides the eight per cent. as interest on the sum advanced, the Bank received $20,000 a year as the expense of management.

The capital is now $72,765,000, *all of which is lent to the Government* at a rate of about three per cent. per annum, and yet it pays a dividend of *seven* per cent.! Its notes are a legal tender, except at its own counter, and it is the only joint stock bank which can issue notes in, or within sixty-five miles of it, or can draw or accept bills of exchange on London. It receives the public revenues, and holds the deposits of the various public offices—being not less than $20,000,000. For discharging these duties and registering transfers and paying the dividends on the public debt, it now receives $640,000. It is a close corporation, managed by twenty-four directors, *who furnish no accounts* to the proprietors. Eight go out every year and eight come in. When the period of election draws near, the directors make out what is termed a house list, giving the names of those whom they wish to have as colleagues, and this list is uniformly elected. *This body is absolute in the extreme, and perfectly free to act as it sees fit under all circumstances. It is led by no authority and restrained by no responsibility.*

The following table, carefully prepared from the official data, shows the amount of Exchequer bills and public deposits held by the Bank of England, the bank notes in circulation, the commercial bills discounted by the bank, and the actual taxation from 1808 to 1831:

|  | Exchequer Bills | Public Deposit | Circulation | Bills Discount'd | Actual Taxation |
|---|---|---|---|---|---|
| 1808 | $74,781,970 | $58,807,240 | $85,556,450 | $64,750,500 | $310,733,605 |
| 1809 | 76,538,865 | 55,468,240 | 97,870,900 | 77,377,500 | 349,399,410 |
| 1810 | 85,983,385 | 59,750,233 | 123,969,950 | 100,353,000 | 339,127,985 |
| 1811 | 109,421,240 | 50,959,270 | 116,534,250 | 71,777,000 | 326,355,500 |
| 1812 | 105,825,950 | 51,950,650 | 115,134,400 | 71,458,000 | 323,760,625 |
| 1813 | 127,956,800 | 51,967,020 | 124,140,600 | 61,651,000 | 241,514,300 |
| 1814 | 174,912,425 | 60,791,135 | 341,141,450 | 66,429,000 | 351,201,765 |
| 1815 | 130,970,430 | 58,687,180 | 136,243,350 | 74,735,500 | 355,015,710 |
| 1816 | 130,487,155 | 54,038,300 | 133,793,600 | 57,082,000 | 313,203,355 |
| 1817 | 135,491,190 | 43,495,655 | 147,718,900 | 19,803,000 | 260,678,745 |
| 1818 | 136,285,060 | 35,334,435 | 131,010,750 | 21,826,000 | 269,836,090 |
| 1819 | 127,095,740 | 22,684,865 | 126,263,420 | 32,575,000 | 256,455,540 |
| 1820 | 95,869,985 | 18,567,210 | 121,496,700 | 19,418,000 | 275,319,465 |
| 1821 | 78,764,765 | 19,600,785 | 111,476,500 | 13,388,500 | 277,650,365 |
| 1822 | 68,344,795 | 20,589,265 | 87,323,950 | 16,833,500 | 226,278,072 |
| 1823 | 59,313,385 | 27,633,175 | 96,156,200 | 15,619,000 | 272,234,845 |
| 1824 | 73,245,935 | 36,110,835 | 100,660,600 | 19,849,000 | 277,282,375 |
| 1825 | 87,072,830 | 20,786,570 | 96,994,200 | 24,607,500 | 268,857,500 |
| 1826 | 87,569,405 | 21,071,355 | 107,817,800 | 24,541,500 | 156,574,650 |
| 1827 | 99,047,975 | 21,119,335 | 213,788,000 | 6,222,000 | 256,558,585 |
| 1828 | 103,413,880 | 19,108,485 | 106,787,550 | 5,317,000 | 263,715,950 |
| 1829 | 100,362,200 | 19,313,280 | 97,786,900 | 11,253,500 | 251,188,915 |
| 1830 | 104,558,080 | 23,809,760 | 107,223,500 | 4,599,500 | 253,541,925 |
| 1831 | 92,282,760 | 19,700,510 | 92,633,150 | 7,668,000 | 233,097,870 |
|  | $2,451,493,265 | $877,252,000 | $2,720,183,100 | $881,449,500 | $7,330,022,260 |

PUBLIC CREDIT BETTER THAN THE NOTES OF THE BANK.

By reference to Mr. Calhoun's speeches, as quoted, it will be seen that North Carolina maintained for years a circulation of irredeemable paper money of four times the sum of the annual taxation, which did not depreciate, although it was not a legal tender; the value being maintained by the fact that it was receivable at par with gold in the payment of taxes; and also, that Russia, upon a current revenue of ninety millions of dollars, sustained, at par with gold, a current circulation of irredeemable paper of one hundred and twenty millions of dollars. Is it not apparent that, if instead

of borrowing the credit of the Bank, the Government of England had issued its certificates, receivable in the payment of taxes and fundable at a proper rate of interest, the value of the public credit would have been equal to the value of the notes of the Bank of England? The table shows that the annual average of the Exchequer bills held by the Bank, and upon which Government paid interest, was ...... .............................$102,145,552
and the average public deposits was....................................  35,552,166
and the average sum of taxes was................................ 305,446,758

making a fund of...........,........................................$444,144,476
placed by the Government with the Bank as its agent, and which sum was used by the Bank as the basis of its issues. If the Government had applied these resources to sustain its own credit, and that credit had been made a legal tender, instead of making the notes of the Bank a tender, inasmuch as the public credit of England would not have been subject to the laws which regulate the export and import of specie, the quantity of the public credit, in circulation, could have been regulated by Parliament; and the value of the currency would have been much more uniform and stable than it has been under the regulations of the Bank. Is it not also apparent that, in that case, there would have been no such fluctuations in the quantity and values of money and of credit; no such suspensions of banks; no such depreciations in the values of property and of labor; and no such individual distress and bankruptcies as the management of that Bank has caused, not only in England, but throughout the commercial world?

Why did the Government pay interest on the EXCHEQUER BILLS? Was it not because these bills, instead of being a tender, represented the unfunded debt, and the payment of interest was necessary to make them of equal value as bank notes, which were a tender? If so, by making the public credit, issued as certificates, receivable in payment of taxes, a tender (that is, converting them into money), the payment of interest would no longer be requisite to maintain the value of so much as was requisite for use as money? And who, with our own experience, will deny that Parliament could, by a judicious system of taxing the unfunded certificates, cause all to be funded, except the sum requisite for use as money? Is it not further apparent that such a use of the public credit would save to the people and the Government the whole of the interest on the sum used as currency? If we assume that the sum thus used would be no more than the annual taxes, as this average, as given in the table, was $305,446,758, the interest upon that sum, at three per cent. only, would be an annuity of $9,163,402.74, which, if compounded at three per cent., would create a sinking fund which would soon absorb the whole public debt of England! This, however, is apart from the ruinous effect which the management of the Bank has had, and will have, upon individual credit and upon the progress of individual industry and the general prosperity of this country.

That England herself is not satisfied with that system appears in the fact stated by Hardcastle, in his treatise upon Banks and Bankers, that the bare titles of the acts of Parliament passed upon the subject of the affairs of the bank "occupy more than 200 pages of the index of the statutes at large."

Surely there must be some defect in a system which requires so much tinkering—and I, for one, am unwilling that the tinkers who have so botched their own system shall be permitted to regulate ours. And that is the very danger which threatens us.

Let me be distinctly understood. I do not complain of or censure the bank as a bank. It is not the bank, but the system as regulated by Parliament, and those who manage the bank under that system, which I believe rests upon three fundamental errors.

1st. That the paper circulation should at no time exceed the value of the gold and silver of which it supplies the place.

2d. That the paper circulation should depend upon the quantity of the bullion in the Bank and be regulated by the foreign Exchange.

3d. That whenever there is a foreign demand for gold, the Bank, by refusing to discount commercial paper, and the sale of Exchequer bills, shall diminish the quantity of bank paper in circulation, and so increase the demand for gold, as a means of payment, as to render gold of more value in England than it may be in the country to which it may have gone, and thus coerce its reflux to the Bank.

These, we believe, are fundamental principles in the management of the Bank, and we believe them to be fundamental errors, as the history of the Bank and of the world, so far as the world has been under the influence of the bank, demonstrates. This error is the more striking, when we take into consideration the causes which induce the export of gold. In case of wars, gold may be in greater demand elsewhere, and being at a premium, will be sent abroad. In case of foreign loans, a premium will be given which will cause it to be exported. In case of bad harvests, foreign wheat must be paid for in gold. In all such cases the bank refuses to renew discounts. If this does not produce a sufficient pressure, then she goes into the market, sells Exchequer bills in exchange for bank notes, and thus renders the demand for gold so severe as to compel the reflux. That some idea may be formed of the effect of this turning of the bank screw, I quote from Hardcastle. He says:

Our banking system is bad in the extreme; it has been everything by turns, but what it ought to be, and nothing long. It is not only bad itself, but it communicates evil to everything around it. It is an epidemic that arrests and affects all classes; a plague that corrupts and kills high and low, poor and affluent, without distinction—a thousand incidents have taken place in this city within a year [London in 1842] which exhibit our monetary affairs in a most deplorable condition. . . . . . I have seen, last spring, a bill broker go from house to house, of an afternoon, with the bills of a country bank, accepted by first rate firms in Lombard street, and cash could not be got for them at five per cent. interest and one and a half per cent. commission. I have known, about the same time, a man with £10,000 Exchequer bills, unable to raise £4,000 upon them at his banker's, and that bank one of the best in Lombard street. I have known a city banker, at the beginning of last year, confess, in a mixed company, that he would be glad to allow ten per cent. for money for six months to come. At the same time, I have known another banker in Lombard street pay eight per cent. for an advance of money on Exchequer bills; and ten per cent. to be charged on the discount of a bill of Exchange, the acceptor of which was then, and still is, a Bank Director. These are facts that tell the true story of our banking system—these are realities that prove our distress. . . . . . . While they last, credit is prostrate, labor fails of its market, and property almost ceases to be wealth. . . . . . Our currency has resembled the shifting sands that impede the navigation of some of our most capacious harbors, and

defy the skill of the most experienced mariners. We have been dealing with a series of experiments, and each succeeding writer has distinguished himself by showing where and how it was that the last experiment had proved a particular failure. . . . . .
The Bank of England had the complete control and absolute management of the finances of the whole country, and the losses which the country has now, for fifty years or so, sustained by repeated abuses of that currency in the hands of the Bank, have been incalculable; so wild and extravagant have been the alternate expansions and contractions; so suddenly and capriciously have the value of money and prices been jerked up and tossed down, that it is not unreasonable to compare the Bank Directors to a set of awkward showmen at a fair, with the trading interests of the nation in a great ill-contrived swing-swong, which at one moment they fling up high in the sky, and at another bring down so low as to drag the ground and rake the gutters with it. . . . . . .
The habit of tampering with the currency was contracted by these gentlemen at an early period. We can trace it distinctly as far back as 1782, and find it persevered in up to 1839, invariably with the same pernicious results. . . . . . A heavy panic, fraught with great commercial distress, ran through the years 1783 and 1784, which has been brought home to the Bank by more than one conclusive witness.
 . . . . . In 1814, the Dutch ports were opened, the harvest was deficient; and that most searching of the calamities, to which our artificial condition is exposed, no sooner visited the land, than the importation of foreign corn occasioned a great decline in the price of this principal article of agricultural produce, which gradually extended to the price of commodities generally   Unprecedented suffering now took place; the storm swept the country through, and raged with increasing violence until 1819, by which time the agricultural and banking interests generally were reduced to the lowest pitch of distress. Farmers were insolvent everywhere; mercantile firms became bankrupt by thousands and levelled their connexions indiscriminately in the dust; whilst as to the bankers, between those who either partially suspended business or wholly broke, in the years 1815 or 1816, there was a diminution of no less than 240 firms. . . . .
In noticing the moving causes of the calamities of 1816, we should bear in mind that the cessation of hostilities on the continent was an established condition of the long promised resumption of cash payments. Much of the panic then existing is referable to a proposal for carrying that measure into effect, in 1818.
The Bank made some preparations for the change by a partial contraction of its issues. But the depression of all the leading interests of the country was too intense, and the notion was quickly abandoned.

He quotes Mr. Atwood, in 1818, as saying:

In the midst of this fall of prices, what operation in business could proceed without loss or ruin? There has been no firm in which the capital of the merchant, none in which the capital of the manufacturer, could be invested without the half of it being sacrificed during this calamitous period. We have been thrown back upon a condition of events in which all industry and enterprize have been rendered pernicious or ruinous, and where no property has been safe, unless hoarded in the shape of money, or lent to others on double security.

He quotes further from Mr. Atwood's evidence before a committee:

The reward of labor being destroyed, the laborers, who can each produce four times as much of the comforts of life as they and their families could possibly consume, are starving while superabundance reigns around them. They find no employment, because the organ of industry, which is money, does not exist in sufficient quantities to give productive classes a reward for their exertions. The peasant idly wanders about, and looks over the hedge of the uncultivated farm, where the land is suffering for want of his labor, but at the same time the farmer has neither the profit nor the labor to bring the land into cultivation.

Speaking of the crisis in 1836, Hardcastle says:

Of the bankruptcies that then took place, and of the extreme depression of our manufactures and commerce, it would be impossible to give any exact account. Prices fell forty per cent. In the manufacturing districts there was no employment for the workmen; merchants stopped payment in numbers, not because they were insolvent and had no property, but because no market was to be had for their goods, no discount for their bills, no advance upon their stocks. It was a rare and melancholy sight to behold English merchants going through the *Gazette* in numbers, while their warehouses were full of commodities, and their characters unimpeached for knowledge of business, integrity and exemplary conduct; yet such were the incidents that characterized the panic of 1836.

. . . . . . There was another panic in 1839 which may be said to have extended itself by a series of fits and convulsions all through the years 1840 and 1841, at which date our commercial system was reduced to the lowest ebb of distress. The number of banks which stopped or disappeared during this interval was unusually great, the difficulty of getting money as rigid as ever, and the stagnation of our commerce, the scarcity of good mercantile paper, extreme. . . . . . . Late in 1840 began the storm which, continuing to rage all through 1841, and not even as yet (in 1842) blown over, has swept away, during its protracted and ruinous course, an unusual number of banking establishments. A history of these misfortunes, in their various details, is here out of the question; to trace the separate cases to their source, and detail at length their consequences, would fill a volume, and then, in all probability, leave the subject unexhausted I had prepared a summary of the losses occasioned by the different failures amongst the private and joint stock banks during the last two years, but the amount appears so formidably large on the one side and so small on the other, that it would be invidious to publish it.

The cause of these disasters are explained by the eminent banker, Jones Loyd, who, speaking of the crisis of 1840, said :

Against the actual exhaustion of its treasure by a drain through the foreign exchanges, the bank, under almost any circumstances, has the power of protecting herself; but to do this she must produce upon the money market a pressure ruinous from its suddenness and severity; she must save herself by the destruction of all around her.

I have said that, among other causes, the creation of foreign loans in England will cause a demand for bullion for export, and, consequently, cause fluctuations in the quantity and value of money, and, in proof of this, I refer to

### THE CRISIS OF 1820 AND 1826.

If we recur to the history of the times it will do much to establish the truth of the arguments, and to enforce the necessity of adopting the measures which I propose as the only means of preventing the frequent recurrence of the overwhelming disasters which have fallen upon the commercial world, and especially upon the United States, as the consequence of the demand for specie, created by the measures and policy of the Bank of England.

To supply the Government of the United States with funds to prosecute the war of 1812, the Banks in the Southern and Western States were compelled to suspend specie payment. Congress in 1816 chartered the Bank of the United States as a means of aiding, or rather of coercing, the resumption of specie payments. The Indian title to large tracts of fertile lands was extinguished by the peace, which lands were immediately surveyed and put upon the market. The notes of the suspended banks were received in payment for these lands and for duties; these notes were placed in the Bank of the United States as Government deposits, and by that Bank presented to the local Banks for specie. Sir Robert Peel's bill requiring the Bank of England to resume specie payment of her one pound notes in 1822, and generally in 1825, passed in 1819, the consequence was that the specie which was thus withdrawn from the local banks by the Bank of the United States, was withdrawn from that Bank by the operations of commerce and remitted to England, until, in Au-

gust; 1825, the specie in the Bank of England had increased to more than seventy-five millions of dollars. But the pressure created by the Bank of the United States upon the local banks had been such, and the opposition to the Bank became so great in Virginia, Maryland, Tennessee, Kentucky, Ohio, and other Southern and Western States, that it was arranged between Mr. Cheves, then the President of the Bank, and Mr. Crawford, the Secretary of the Treasury, that large sums were left on deposit with certain selected local banks, upon condition that they would convert the notes of other local banks into specie, to be by them deposited in the Bank of the United States. Thus, the Banks of Edwardsville in Illinois, and of Missouri at St. Louis, being on opposite sides of the river, were each made depositaries, with large standing deposits, upon condition that they would cash the notes of each other and remit, by the same steamer, the specie thus obtained to the Branch of the United States Bank in Louisville, Kentucky. Mr. Cheves, then the President of the Bank, in a Report to the Stockholders, in 1822, says: "The specie in the vaults at the close of the day, on the 1st of April, 1819, was only 126,745 dollars and 28 cents, and the Bank owed to the City Banks, deducting balances due to it, 79,125 dollars and 99 cents. It is true, there were in the mint 267,978 dollars and 9 cents, and in transitu from Kentucky and Ohio, overland, $250,000; but the Treasury dividends were payable on that day to the amount of near 500,000 dollars, and there remained at the close of the day more than one half the sum subject to draft. * * * *
On the 12th of the same month, the Bank had in its vaults but 71,522 dollars and 47 cents, and owed to the City Banks a balance of 196,148 dollars and 47 cents; exceeding the specie in its vaults 124,895 dollars and 19 cents. * * * * The Bank in this situation, the office in New York was little better, and the office in Boston a great deal worse. At the same time, the Bank owed to Baring Brothers & Co., and to Thos. Wilson & Co., nearly 900,000 dollars, which it was bound to pay immediately, and which was a charge upon its vaults to that amount. It had, including the notes of its offices, a circulation of six millions of dollars."

The effect of this pressure was another suspension of specie payments, and a depreciation of more than fifty per cent. of the exchangeable values of property, and the Government of the United States was compelled to compromise with the purchasers of public lands on the deferred payments, allowing them to consolidate their payments theretofore made at the rate of less than fifty cents on the dollar. That is, a party who had purchased lands and paid ten thousand dollars, owing thirty thousand, was permitted to relinquish lands to the amount of thirty thousand dollars in payment of his debt, and apply the ten thousand paid, at the rate of less than fifty cents on the dollar, in payment for lands not relinquished. Such were the effects, in England and in the United States, of the delusion which enforced the necessity of maintaining a specie currency. And for whose benefit? Did it benefit the people, or the Government of England, or of the United States? No; for inasmuch as the delay in the resumption of specie payment by the Bank of England, and the large amount of its paper in circulation, enabled the country banks and private bankers greatly to increase their issues, the effect was to beget in England a spirit of speculation, which embraced not only large foreign loans, but ran into the working of foreign mines and other visionary and delusive schemes.

The Edinburgh *Review*, of 1826, gives a table showing in detail the sums advanced by England on loans to Prussia, Spain, Naples, Denmark, Columbia, Chili, Poyais, Peru, Portugal, Austria, Greece, Buenos Ayres, Brazil, Mexico, Guatemala, Guadalaxara, which, with other advances on French, Russian and American securities, made the sum $522,692,500 advanced by England, on foreign account, during the eight years, from 1818 to 1825, inclusive. It is apparent that the advances made upon these loans must have created an extraordinary demand for specie in England, and it is obvious that, as the loss of five and a half millions of dollars, in 1857, by the banks of New York, created results so disastrous, as described by Gibbon, the export of so large an amount to pay off the foreign loans, produced the overwhelming losses, bankruptcies and distress so forcibly referred to by Hardcastle and the Edinburgh and London *Quarterly Reviews*, and that that monetary crisis was caused by the fact that the currency of England was convertible into specie, and that the demand for specie thus produced, compelled the bank, to use the words of Jones Loyd, quoted above, to " save herself by the destruction of all around her."

I give the following from the London *Quarterly*, of September, 1832, illustrating the effect of changing a paper into a metallic currency: " As a single specimen of the condition of our internal trade, we give the memorial of the iron and coal masters of Shropshire, Staffordshire and Wales, presented to Earl Grey by a deputation in October last, after being signed by more than three-fourths of the trade in those great manufacturing districts."

We, the undersigned, iron masters and coal masters of the Staffordshire iron and coal districts, think it our duty respectfully to represent to His Majesty's Government the following facts:

1. That for the last five years, ever since what is called the panic of 1825, we have found, with very slight intermissions, a continually increasing depression in the prices of the products of industry, and more particularly in those of pig and bar iron, which have fallen respectively, from upward of 8l. per ton to under 3l. per ton, and from £15 per ton to under £5 per ton.

2. Against this alarming and long continued depression, we have used every possible effort in our power to make bread. We have practiced all manner of economy, and have had recourse to every possible improvement in the working of our mines and manufactories. Our workmen's wages have in many instances been reduced, and such reduction has been attended with, and effected by, very great distress; but the royalties, rents, contracts, and other engagements, under which we hold our respective works and mines, have scarcely been reduced at all, nor can we get them effectually reduced, because the law enforces the payment in full.

3. The prices of the products of our industry having thus fallen within the range of the fixed charges and expenses which the law compels us to discharge, the just and necessary profits of our respective trades have ceased to exist, and in many cases a positive loss attends them.

4. Under these circumstances, we have long hesitated in determining what line of conduct our interest and our duties require us to adopt. If we should abandon our respective trades, our large and expensive outlays in machinery and erections must be sacrificed at an enormous loss to ourselves, and our honest and meritorious workmen must be thrown, in thousands, upon parishes already too much impoverished by their present burthens to support them; and, if we should continue our present trades, we see nothing but the prospect of increasing distress and certain ruin to all around us.

5. In our humble opinion, the great cause which has been mainly instrumental in producing this depression and distress in our respective trades, and among the productive classes of the country generally, is the attempt to render the rents, *taxes*, royalties, and

other various engagements and obligations of the country, convertible, by law, into gold, at £3 17s. 10½d. per oz. This low and antiquated price of the metallic standard of value is no longer capable of effecting a just and equitable distribution of our products between the producer and the consumer; it renders incompatible the permanent existence of remunerating prices, without such a reduction of taxation as we cannot hope to see effected in time to afford us any relief—and it thus tends, ultimately and surely, to destroy the industry, and the peace and happiness of the country.

6. That until the establishment of a circulating medium of a character better suited to the various and complicated demands of society, and to the increased transactions and population of the country, and more competent to effect an interchange, and preserve a remunerating level of prices in the products of industry generally, we can see no prospect of any permanent restoration of the prosperity of our trades, or of the country being able to escape the most frightful sufferings and convulsions.

We, therefore, most respectfully, but very earnestly, request the early attention of His Majesty's Government to these great facts and considerations, and we insist that they will recommend to Parliament the speedy establishment of some *just, adequate* and *efficient currency*, which may properly support the trade and commerce of the country, and preserve such a remunerating level of prices as may ensure to the employers of labor the fair and reasonable profits of their capital and industry, as well as the means of paying the just and necessary wages to their workmen.

Such are the views of practical working men in England of the operation of contracting a debt in paper money at the rate of $150 for one hundred, and paying the interest of three per cent. on it in specie. If such was the effect there, what will be the effect here of paying the interest, in specie, on so large a debt as we will have contracted, at the rate of twenty for one? The London *Quarterly* says:

Our country gentlemen must learn to penetrate the arcana of the *Exchanges*, and fathom the depths of the banking system, if they mean to preserve their broad acres from the grasp of the mortgagee, and their title deeds and mansions from the blaze of revolutionary fires. Difficult and obscure, indeed! Yes, the subject is difficult, just as difficult to the public comprehension as is a juggler's trick, by which, with a "heigh, presto!" he conjures the half crown we thought we had safe in our pocket into his own. How the money vanished it is not so easy to say; but it is nevertheless certain that we had it, and ought still to have it, but he has got it. So it was exactly with the currency juggle. Few of the sufferers can explain or understand how it happened, but the fact is very plain to them that they have somehow lost a great deal of money, and other persons have got hold of it. A little consideration, however, may, we think, render the nature of the trick intelligible to the simplest. It is very clear that those who are in business *pay nearly the same sum in taxes,* at present, as when the goods they deal in sold for double their present prices; so that they really pay two hundred weight of wool, or of cheese, or of sugar, or two pieces of cloth, linen, or calico, or two tons of iron or hardware, to the tax gatherer, for one that they formerly paid; and the taxes, *reckoned in goods,* which is the only sure way of knowing their cost to the producers of goods, by whom they are paid, are clearly twice as high at the end of sixteen years of peace, as they were at the close of a long war! Is it wonderful then that the productive classes are laboring under severe distress! That peace, which usually brings plenty, has thrown away her emblematic horn, and selected hunger for her motto! And can there be any doubt that the fall in prices, which has wrought this fearful evil, is the necessary result, foretold by ourselves and many others at the time, of the legislation of 1819 and 1826, which, by crippling the banking system of England and attempting a currency of *dear metal* for one of *cheap paper,* has caused a continually increasing scarcity of money and contraction of credit!

If we succeed in showing that the unjust restrictions, kept up by the present laws, on the circulating medium of exchange, have had the effect, within a few years past, of silently but forcibly transferring a vast amount of property from the possession of one class to that of another, who had no just right or title to it—of covertly despoiling, in short, one portion of the community, namely: the persons engaged in industry, for the benefit of another portion, the owners of fixed money obligations, payable out of the labor and capital of the former—it will be acknowledged that, until the laws which have perpetuated and continue to sanction this wholesale swindling are repealed, there is no safety for property ; nor can there be any reliance on the stability of those institutions, of which a confidence in the security of property is the indispensable foundation.

Remarking upon the Staffordshire memorial, the *Review* says :
The sufferers here most correctly attribute their losses to the late increase in the value of money, but they seem to look for relief in a deterioration of the standard. In this view we do not concur with them, only because we think so desperate a remedy is not necessary, for that other and unexceptionable plans may be resorted to for the relief of industry. . . . . Next to a direct increase of the supply of the precious metals, the most obvious resource seems to be to augment the efficiency of that which we possess, by a degradation of the standard—in other words, by diminishing the intrinsic value of the coinage; cutting, for instance, our sovereigns, shillings and other pieces of money, into two or more parts, which should each, by law, retain the nominal value of the whole. This is, in substance, the proposal which seems to find most favor with the persons who have spoken or written on the subject of the currency for some years past. It is this, as we have seen, that is advocated by the iron trade, and by their powerful champions, the Messrs. Atwood. It is this to which Mr. Weston, and a large body of agriculturalists have been long pointing as the only practicable mode of permitting them to come to an equitable adjustment with their creditors, *public* and private. . . . .
. . . . We acknowledge, indeed, the force of the retorts levelled by the advocates of this alteration against their opponents, when the necessity of preserving the national faith inviolate is thrown in their teeth. They ask, with bitterness, and with justice, too:
"Is faith to be kept only with the monied interests? Was no good faith to be kept with the landholder, the merchant, the manufacturer, the vast laboring population who bore the weight of the national struggle, who cheerfully made great and numerous sacrifices during the war, and who continue the real strength and greatness of the Kingdom? *No faith whatever was kept with them.* They, through their representatives, engaged themselves to a debt of so many pound *notes*—but not to the same number of sovereigns—to a debt consisting of money, *at its then value*, but they protest being held responsible for the same annual sum now that its value has been artificially *doubled*. Does not good faith require that the scale should be held fairly between debtor and creditor ? Was it consistent with the national faith, upon the plea of arresting the progress of depreciation in 1819, to turn the tables wholly the other way, and, by reviving an obsolete standard, to give to monied obligations a value *that is a command over the produce and property of others*, which the persons originally forming those contracts could never have contemplated, and which consigned at once to overwhelming and unmerited ruin, the commerce, the manufactures and agriculture of the empire?"
We freely admit the weight of these remonstrances. We acknowledge that, through an overstrained anxiety for observing the letter of the national faith, the spirit of the obligation was disregarded and a gross injustice committed on the great body of producers throughout the Kingdom, as well as on all debtors. It is true—
" Nothing could be more honorable than the feeling which induced our statesmen to return to the ancient standard ; but, to our sorrow, their estimate of its effects was much below the mark. They did not see what a revolution of property would ensue. They consulted our honor, our reputed solvency, but not our real means. Mr. Ricardo told them the change would be five per cent. Events have proved it fifty. . . . . . .
There remains another course for consideration; one which we have urged for some time past upon the public, as the true mode of relief from our monetary difficulties. . . . . . . We mean the removal of the mischievous restrictions which now fetter the circulation of credit through this country, and the concession of the free right of commerce to provide itself with whatever instruments it may require for effecting its exchanges uninterfered with by those officious legislative intermeddlings which experience has sufficiently proved to be fatal to almost everything they touch, but to nothing so much so as to the currency. It is physically impossible to carry on the commerce of the civilized world by the aid of a purely metallic currency—no, not though our gold and silver coins were every tenth year debased to a tenth ! Why, in London alone, five

millions sterling ($25,000,000) are daily exchanged at the Clearing House in the course of a few hours. We should like to see the attempt made to bring this infinity of transactions to a settlement in coined money. Credit money, in some shape or other, always has, and must have, performed the part of a circulating medium to a very considerable extent. And (by one of those wonderful compensatory processes which so frequently claim the admiration of every investigation of civil as well as of physical economy) there is in the nature of credit an elasticity which causes it, when left unshackled by law, to adapt itself to the necessities of commerce and the legitimate demands of the market. . . . . . The only measures which appear to us to be needed upon the expiration of the Bank Charter, are: 1st. That all banks be required to deposit security in Government stock to the full amount of the notes they issue. 2d. That the law be repealed which forbids the issue of notes under five pounds. 3d. We would make the notes of *metropolitan banks only* convertible into bars of bullion, on the plan of Mr. Ricardo, and allow the notes of country banks to be paid in those of the metropolitan banks."

The following table, compiled from data, given by John Taylor, Jr., and Ayres' *Financial Register*, gives the amount of debt bonded, the equivalent in three per cent. consols, the stock created for one hundred pounds in money, the highest and the lowest prices for consols, and the market value of paper currency per cent., from 1800 to 1824, inclusive:

| Years | Amount of Debt Bonded | Equivalent in 3 per cent. Bonds | Stock created for £100 in Money | The Highest Price | The Lowest Price | Market value of paper currency per cent. |
|---|---|---|---|---|---|---|
| 1800 | £20,500,000 | £32,185,000 | £158 50d. | 67½ | 60 | £100 00s. 2d. |
| 1801 | 36,910,000 | 63,578,100 | 174 54 | 70 | 54¼ | 91 12 6 |
| 1802 | 25,000,000 | 32,990,630 | 132 17 | 79 | 66 | 91 14 2 |
| 1803 | 12,000,000 | 20,483,330 | 173 55 | 75 | 50¼ | 97 6 10 |
| 1804 | 14,500,000 | 26,390,000 | 185 00 | 56¾ | 53¾ | 97 6 10 |
| 1805 | 22,500,000 | 41,800,000 | 177 20 | 62 | 57 | 97 6 10 |
| 1806 | 20,000,000 | 33,200,000 | 167 70 | 64⅜ | 58¼ | 97 6 10 |
| 1807 | 15,700,000 | 24,798,290 | 159 20 | 64⅜ | 57⅞ | 97 6 10 |
| 1808 | 14,500,000 | 23,530,622 | 162 67 | 69⅝ | 22⅜ | 97 6 10 |
| 1809 | 22,532,100 | 35,218,740 | 161 39 | 70⅜ | 63⅝ | 97 6 10 |
| 1810 | 21,711,000 | 33,112,106 | 152 67 | 71 | 63¼ | 97 6 10 |
| 1811 | 24,000,000 | 39,724,620 | 166 53 | 66¾ | 61⅛ | 86 10 6 |
| 1812 | 34,721,325 | 57,198,380 | 180 00 | 63 | 55¼ | 92 3 2 |
| 1813 | 64,755,700 | 118,736,690 | 184 87 | 67½ | 54¼ | 79 5 3 |
| 1814 | 24,007,400 | 36,839,930 | 154 17 | 72¼ | 61½ | 77 2 0 |
| 1815 | 54,135,589 | 102,787,340 | 191 52 | 65⅜ | 57¼ | 74 16 6 |
| 1816 | | | | 64⅜ | 59¼ | 83 5 8 |
| 1817 | | | | 62 | 62 | 79 6 10 |
| 1818 | | | | 72 | 73 | 95 11 0 |
| 1819 | | | | 79 | 64¾ | 97 8 0 |
| 1820 | | | | 70¼ | 65⅝ | 106 0 0 |
| 1821 | | | | 78¼ | 68¼ | 100 0 0 |
| 1822 | | | | 83 | 75⅜ | 100 0 0 |
| 1823 | | | | 85¾ | 72 | 100 0 0 |
| 1824 | | | | 96⅝ | 84¼ | 100 0 0 |
| Total, | £427,473,114 | £723,570,672 | | | | |
| Av'rage | | | £167 60 | 73 | 63 | £93 15s. 1d. |

* It will be seen that, although the Bank of England suspended payment in 1797, the notes were at par with gold in 1800 and again in 1820, and continued at par until it resumed payment in 1825, the average depreciation during the suspension being less than seven per cent. It is a striking fact

that the greater part of this depreciation was during the years from 1810 to 1815, inclusive, when the loans and subsidies given to her allies, and the expenditures of the French war, created an extraordinary demand for specie to be disbursed on the continent (these loans and subsidies amounting to the enormous sum of $301,047,813!!!).

McCulloch, in a note (p. 78), says:

So early as December, 1794, the Court of Directors (of the Bank) represented to Government their uneasiness on account of the debt due by the Government to the Bank, and anxiously requested a repayment of at least a considerable part of what had been advanced. In January, 1795, they resolved to limit their advances upon Treasury bills to £500,000; and, at the same time, they informed Mr. Pitt that it was their wish that he would adjust his measures for the year, *in such a manner, as not to depend on any assistance from them.* On the 11th of February, 1796, they resolved, "*that it is the opinion of this Court, founded upon the experience of the late Imperial loan, that if any further loan or advance of money to the Emperor, or to any of the foreign States, should, in the present state of affairs, take place, it will, in all probability, prove fatal to the Bank of England.*"

If we recur to the value of money, as compared with the value of the mass of circulating commodities, it will be seen that this difference between the value of bank notes (paper money) and specie indicates an increased value of the precious metals rather than a decreased value of paper money.

By reference to the table given above, it will be seen that, in 1814, the public credit was depreciated nearly 84 per cent., and that the value of paper, as compared with gold, fluctuated between 72½ and 61½ per cent., and yet, the Edinburgh *Review*, speaking of the effect of the causes then operating on prices in England, says:

The bank failures that then occurred were the more distressing, as they chiefly affected the industrious classes, and frequently swallowed up in an instant the fruits of a long life of unremitting and laborious exertion. Thousands upon thousands, who had, in 1813, considered themselves as affluent, found they were destitute of all real property, and sunk, as if by enchantment and without any fault of their own, into the abyss of poverty! The late Mr. Horner, the accuracy and extent of whose information on such subjects will not be disputed, stated in his place in the House of Commons, that the destruction of the country bank paper, in 1815 and 1816, had given rise to an universality of wretchedness and misery, which had never been equalled, except, perhaps, by the breaking up of the Mississippi scheme in France.

Engaged, as England was, in a struggle upon which, as she believed, depended her maritime and commercial supremacy, she was compelled to advance loans and subsidies to her allies, and hence we find that the Bank was allowed to suspend specie payment in 1797, and that in the years 1814 and 1815 England advanced, in loans and subsidies, to Spain, Portugal, Sicily, Sweden, Russia, Prussia, Austria, *France,* Hanover, Denmark, and other minor Powers of the Continent, £19,366,307 15s. 9d. (or $96,831,539), and it is, therefore, apparent, that inasmuch as the current expenditures of the British army on the Continent, as well as these large loans and subsidies, were paid in specie, the demand for specie to meet these payments caused the relative depreciation of bank notes, the fall of prices, the destruction of the country banks, and the consequent failures, bankruptcies and distress. Had England used her credit, as I propose, instead of using the Bank credit, there would have been no such failures of her banks and no such fall of prices or depreciation of the values of property. Is it not obvious that, inasmuch as the whole capital of the Bank consisted of the public credit, the Government, having the power of taxing and funding, could have purchased gold at the same price, or less, than that which the bank paid for it? Why, then, did the Government give her credit bearing interest in exchange for bank notes bearing no interest?

As bank notes were not current on the continent the Government could not pay the loans and subsidies to their allies in bank notes, and were, therefore, compelled to give a premium for gold; and hence the depreciation of bank notes as compared with gold.

### PAPER MONEY.

McCulloch, in his article upon the general principles of banking, says:

Every country has a certain number of exchanges to make; and whether these are effected by the employment of a given number of coins of a particular denomination, or by the employment of the same number of notes of the same denomination, is, in this respect, of no importance whatever. Notes which have been made a legal tender, and are not payable on demand, do not circulate because they are of the same real value as the commodities for which they are exchanged, but they circulate because having been selected to perform the functions of money, they are as such received by all individuals in payment of their debts. Notes of this description may be regarded as a sort of tickets or counters to be used in computing the value of property, and in transferring it from one individual to another. And as they are nowise affected by fluctuations of credit, their value, it is obvious, must depend entirely on the quantity of them in circulation as compared with the payments to be made through their instrumentality, or the business they have to perform. By reducing the supply of notes below the supply of coins that would circulate in their place were they withdrawn, *their value is raised above the value of gold;* while by increasing them to a greater extent it is proportionally lowered.

Hence, supposing it were possible to obtain any security other than convertibility into the precious metals, that *notes declared to be a legal tender* would not be issued in excess, but that their number afloat would be so adjusted as to preserve their value as compared with gold nearly uniform, the obligation to pay them on demand might be done away. But it is needless to say that no such security can be obtained. Whenever the power to issue paper, not immediately convertible, has been conceded to *any set of persons* it has been abused, or, which is the same thing, such paper has been uniformly over issued or its value depreciated by excess.

It will be seen that McCulloch's objection to an unconvertible paper is limited to the fact that whenever the power to issue such paper has been conceded *to any set of persons* they have uniformly issued it in excess. It is apparent that he refers to an issue of such paper by banks and bankers, and not to an issue by Government under such a system of taxation and funding as would limit the sum in circulation to the sum wanted as money. I agree that an over issue will depreciate the value of such a paper, and therefore I propose not that it shall be issued by the banks but by the Government, and that the excess be funded, and that the funding shall be coerced by a judicious system of taxing. He adds:

In 1793, 1814, 1815, 1816, and in 1825, a very large proportion of the country banks were destroyed, and produced by their fall an extent of ruin that has hardly been equalled in any other country. And when such disasters have already happened it is surely the bounden duty of Government to hinder by every means in its power their recurrence.

McCulloch was the partisan of the Bank of England, and his remedy for the evils of which he complains was to strengthen that bank by making large bars of gold, instead of the current coins a tender, and to prevent an issue of small notes by the country banks. He believed that the large

dealers would not run upon the bank for specie, and that the holders of small notes were liable to become alarmed and demand payment. His remedy was suspension on small sums and masses of bullion for large. I would recur to the large sums remitted by the Government to the continent, for the support of the armies and in the payment of subsidies, as the cause of the demand for gold in 1814, 1815, and in 1816, and I would explain the monetary crisis of 1825 by the fact that the foreign loans contracted and the vast speculations entered into in England after the war, and before the resumption of specie payments created so great a demand for specie to comply with the engagements then entered into, that the pressure upon the bank and the contraction of the currency below the *specie level* produced then the ruinous depreciation of the values of property as compared with gold. For, as before remarked, it is obvious that it was the increased value of gold, and not the decreased value of bank notes, which caused the disasters so forcibly described. If, instead of placing in the bank an annual average of Exchequer bills of......................................................$102,145,552
and of deposits.................................................................... 36,552,166
and of the public revenue...................................................... 305,446,344

making of public resources...................................................$444,044,062
the Government had issued its own credit, in a shape suitable for currency, *which was a legal tender*, and receivable in payment of the public dues, and fundable at a proper rate of interest and reconvertible into currency, limiting the amount in circulation to the sum requisite for that purpose by a proper system of taxing the excess; and had required each bank to place in the treasury an amount of the reconvertible funded debt as a security for the payment of their notes, there would have been no such speculations in foreign loans; no such depreciation of the value of credit or of property would have then occurred; and consequently there would have been no such bankruptcies and distress. The power to coin money and regulate its value is vested in the British and French Governments as in ours, and as the French *livre* of 1789, contains only the seventy-eighth part of the original *livre* of the year 800, and the English *pound unit* contains but a small fraction more than one-fourth part of the original pound sterling, and the individual obligations, as well as the *public debt* of England, had been contracted when the currency was abundant and cheap, instead of urging the issue of the public credit as money regulated as proposed, an effort was made to reduce the value of the coinage by increasing the alloy or diminishing its weight, and the issue before the British public was the use of bank notes or of a metallic coin thus depreciated, they preferred a bank note convertible into specie; I would restore the value of our currency by making it convertible, not into specie, but into a six per cent. re-convertible bond, and would coerce the conversion by taxing the excess, instead of depreciating the value of metallic coins by increasing the alloy or reducing the weight. Few, I presume, will deny the power of Congress thus to depreciate the coins of gold or silver; and as in that case the depreciated dollar would still be a dollar, it is clearly in the power of Congress to reduce the value of metallic coins much below what would be the value of the currency under the system which I pro-

pose. If the alloy in the metallic coins was so increased, or the weight was so reduced, as that its exchangeable value would be no more than the value of the paper dollar issued by Government, the dollar would be a dollar still, and as much a legal tender as it now is. If Congress can so reduce the value of gold, as a tender, the argument that Congress cannot make paper a tender, because to do so would impair the obligation of contracts, by authorizing payment in a less valuable medium, is untenable. The fallacy of that argument is further illustrated by supposing that A, being indebted to B, has, in his possession, corn, wheat, sugar, beeves, iron, or any other articles liable to be taken for the public use, and upon the sale of which he relies to obtain the means of paying the debt due to B; yet, the Government sends an agent who forcibly takes A's property, and compels him to take Treasury Notes in payment. If the Treasury Notes are a legal tender, they can be used to pay A's debt to B; but if not a tender, and Congress has no power to make them so, upon what principle can the seizure of the property of A be justified? If it be "necessary and proper" to pay A in Treasury Notes, which I maintain it is, certainly it is also "necessary and proper" to enable A to pay his debt in the same money which the Congress have compelled him to receive, for the very purpose of the Constitution was to "establish justice;" and, surely, it is not justice if the Government deprives A of the means of payment, and at the same time arms B with the power of the law to enforce it. The promise of A would be to pay in dollars; Congress has authorized the issue of *paper* dollars, and compels the public creditors to receive them in payment. And why do we permit Congress to do this? Is it not because it is "necessary and proper" for carrying into execution" the powers "vested by the Constitution in the Government of the Confederate States?" If Congress has power to issue and compel the creditors to receive, in payment, a depreciated paper money, surely Congress may pass laws making it a tender to the creditors of those who have been coerced by the Government to receive it; and especially if the effect will be to greatly increase its value when it is used by the Government.

---

## CAN CONGRESS REGULATE THE VALUE OF A METALLIC OR A PAPER CURRENCY CONVERTIBLE INTO GOLD?

It is the duty of Congress to regulate the value of money. Can Congress regulate the value of gold or silver? How, and by what standard, will they measure their value? Sir William Petty said that the day's food of an adult man, and not the day's labor, is the common measure of the value of silver; John Taylor, Jr., says that the corn consumed in the production; and Adam Smith and Ricardo, and the Edinburgh *Review*, say that the labor requisite to produce them is the proper measure of the value of the precious metals. If the value of gold depends upon the value of the day's food, or of the corn consumed, or of the labor expended in producing it, it follows that the value of gold must fluctuate as the value of the food, the corn, or the labor used in producing it may fluctuate. Chivalier says: " If there be anything confirmed by history, it is that the efforts of Government are powerless to regulate the value of gold and silver in relation to other commodities." If Congress cannot regulate the value of gold and silver, it is manifest that they cannot regulate the value of specie or of a paper money convertible into specie. If Congress cannot regulate the value of a metallic currency, because they cannot regulate the cost of gold and silver, the power to regulate its value is rendered more difficult by the fact that, inasmuch as the precious metals are of universal use among all civilized nations, and are easily exported from one nation to any other, the value of metallic money in the Confederate States will be regulated by the contingencies which may effect its value in the foreign markets; which value will be determined by circumstances, over which our Congress can exercise no control. This is further illustrated by the annexed diagrams—for the two first of which I am indebted to Mr. Edward Hazlewood, of London, and for the other to Gibbon's work on the Banks and Banking in New York:

## DIAGRAM

*Showing the Fluctuations in the rate of interest charged by the Bank of England, as regulated by the Amount of Bullion in its vaults, the figures in the margin representing the Bullion in millions of dollars (from $35,000,000 to $100,000,000), and the irregular lines indicating the rates of interest.*

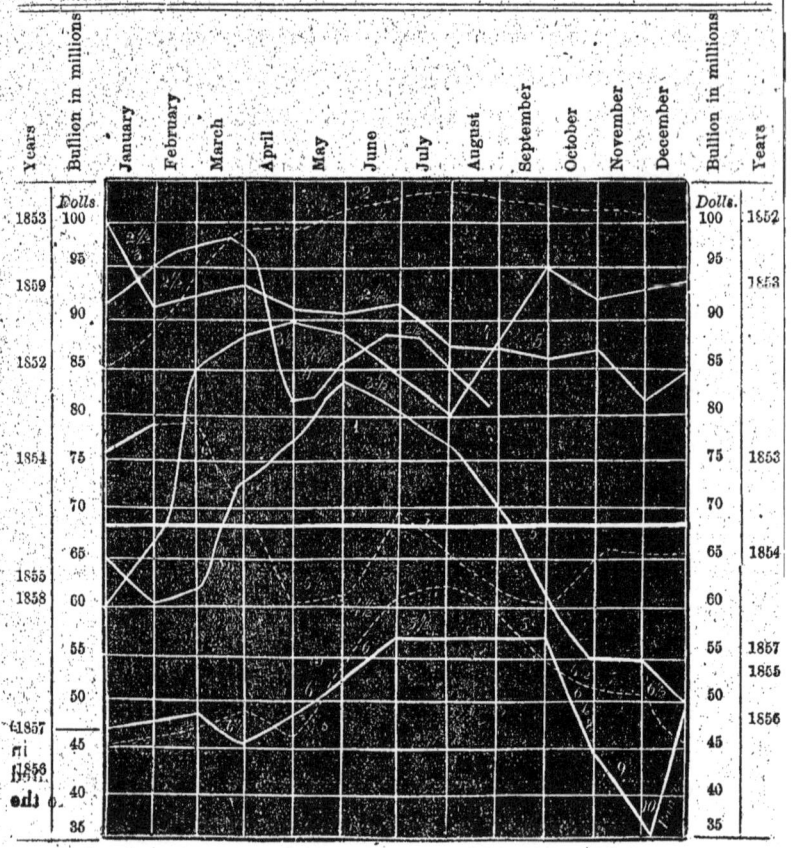

37

# DIAGRAM

Showing the Fluctuations of the Amount of Notes issued by, and of the Liabilities of the Bank of England, for ten years, from 1844 to 1854.

The second represents the liabilities and the issues of the Bank of England from 1844 to 1853, inclusive, the horizontal lines each representing five millions of dollars. Thus, in 1844, the issues of the bank were less than one hundred and forty millions of dollars, and, in 1847, they were less than one hundred and ten millions; and yet, in 1852, they were one hundred and eighty. Now, as the effect of an over-issue of a paper, convertible into specie, is to depreciate the value of the whole currency, gold as well as paper, and consequently to cause the gold to be exported, inasmuch as the issues of the Bank of England are regulated by the quantity of specie in its vaults, it is obvious that the regulation, which requires the Bank to reduce its issues under an unfavorable foreign exchange, and allows an increased issue of bank notes when the exchange is favorable, must, of necessity, create that fluctuation in the value of money and depreciation in the values of property which characterizes the history of British banking and finance.

The pretence of those who manage the Bank is, that they prefer a paper convertible into specie, because it is more stable in value than an inconvertible paper would be. By reference to the first diagram, it will be seen that the figures on the margin represent the years, and the sums of bullion in the Bank; the perpendicular lines the months, and the horizontal lines indicating each five millions of dollars. The irregular lines represent the fluctuations in the quantity of specie in the Bank, whilst the figures on these lines represent the fluctuations in the rates of interest charged by the Bank. Thus, in January, 1852, the bullion in the Bank was eighty-five millions, and in February, interest was 2½ per cent.; in June, the bullion was more than one hundred millions, and interest was but two per cent., whilst in January, 1857, there was in the Bank say forty-six millions, and interest was, in March, 6½ per cent. The bullion rose, in July, to fifty-seven millions, and interest was 5½ per cent. It continued at the same level until October, and interest was 5 per cent.; from October 1st to 10th December, it ran down to thirty-five millions, and interest rose to 6½, 8, 9 and 10 per cent. The effect of the severe pressure for gold in London was a universal panic throughout the commercial world, forcing a current of gold toward the great commercial centres of London, Paris, Vienna and Hamburg. The accumulation at these centres was greatly beyond the sum requisite to maintain the proper specie level. This is forcibly illustrated by the table given on page 14, and by the third diagram, for which I am indebted to Gibbon's work on the "Banks and Banking in New York."

I have explained that the effect of this contraction and expansion of the specie and circulation of the Bank of England, instead of giving uniformity and stability to the monetary system of England, is to cause the most ruinous fluctuation in the values of money and of property, not only in England, but in all other countries having a metallic or convertible paper currency, and having extensive commercial relations with England. The diagrams and statistics, taken from Gibbon's very valuable work, show that, whilst the pressure of the Bank screw in London compelled the Banks of New York to so diminish their discounts as to cause unexampled pecuniary

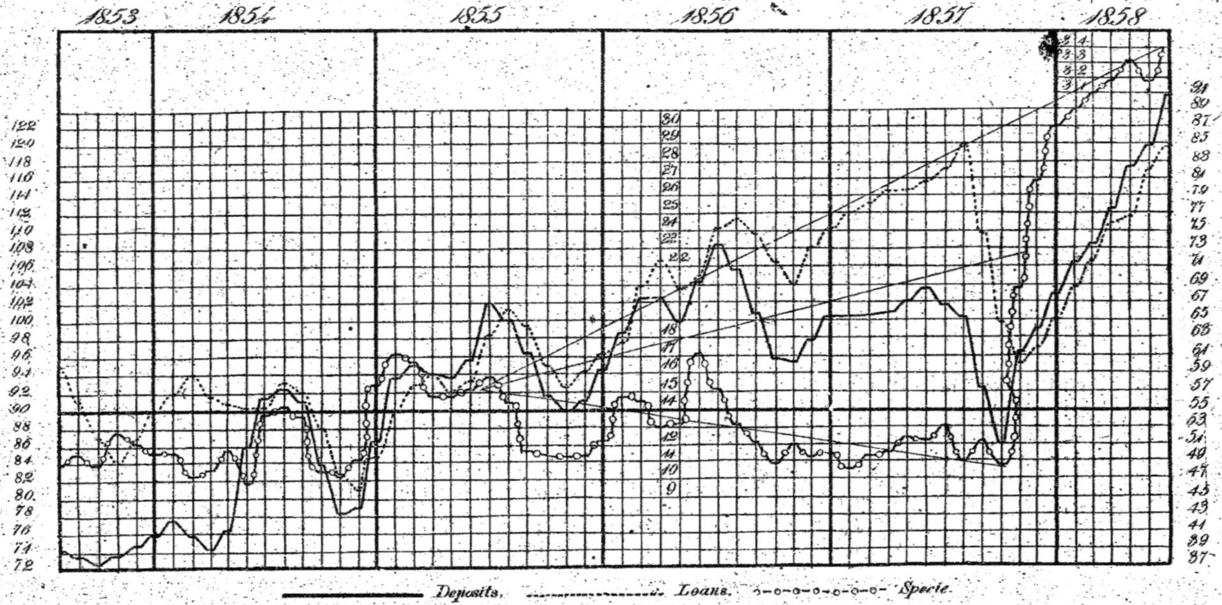
1853
1854
1855
1856
1857
1858
Deposits.
Loans.
Specie.

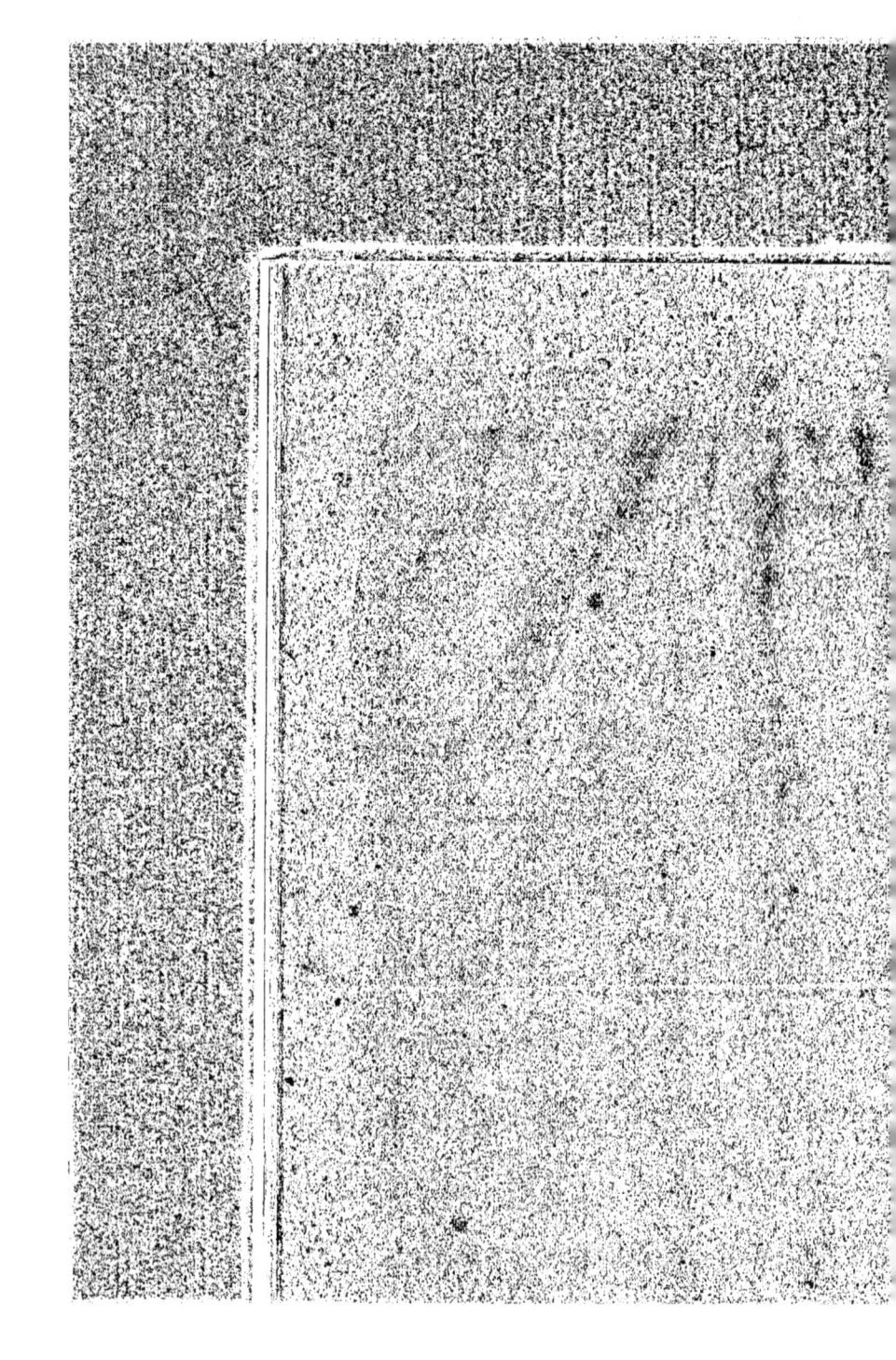

losses and distress, the ultimate effect was to accumulate in the Banks of New York, by force of the reaction, more than three times the sum, in specie, requisite to maintain the value of the credit and circulation of the Banks of New York on a par with specie—demonstrating, beyond question, that the credit of the Banks of New York does not depend upon the specie in their vaults, but upon the securities, consisting of mortgages on real estate, and the bonds of the State and of the United States, deposited with the State as collateral security for the payment of their notes, and upon the solvency of those who deal with the banks, and use the credit and circulation of the banks in their purchases and payments.

The operation of the financial system, predicated on a metallic basis, is this: England, by the magnitude and expansion of her commerce, can create balances in her favor in most of all other countries with whom she trades. By refusing to renew her discount of commercial paper, and by the sale of exchequer bills, the Bank of England can render money so much dearer in London, than it may be elsewhere, as to coerce the greater part of the balances to be paid in specie. Thus say that the commercial balances due to England are $100,000,000, and the demand for specie in payment, brings to London eighty millions of dollars, of which fifty millions are an excess beyond the sum required to reduce the value of money in England to the "proper level," the extra demand having put the precious metals of all other countries in motion towards London, would create an excess greatly beyond the wants of London. The bank, which but yesterday demanded ten per cent., and refused to discount the best commercial paper, even at that rate, to day will be in the market, seeking investment at two per cent.!! Is it surprising that those who regulate the foreign exchange, and make untold profits by the movement of specie, insist upon a specie basis?

It will be impossible to create such a demand for money under the system which I propose. The certificates of our Government, made a legal tender here, will not be a tender in London. They will be money here, but, as they will not be money in London, they cannot be exported to London. With us they may be made equal to gold for the purchase of our exports, and through our exports we can command whatever we may desire of foreign merchandise. Whilst the large sum of the public debt will, as I have said, become the basis of bank issues, the payment of which, being secured by the convertible bonds of the Confederate States, will, at no time, be affected or depreciated by a foreign demand for specie. In that case, specie, like cotton, will be a commodity, the value of which will depend upon the demand for it. If we wish to obtain foreign exchange to pay for British goods, and the British merchants, or the British bankers, or their agents, refuse to take our Treasury certificates in payment, we must give, in exchange for it, our cotton, or some other exportable commodity which we can purchase with our Treasury certificates, or with our bank notes, predicated upon the bonds which represent the certificates that have been funded. If the British gold is worth more than our certificates, then we must demand so much the more for our cotton, if payable in our currency. We must regulate the value of our surplus produce by the relative value of our currency. The value of gold, as compared with silver, is as fifteen to one; yet, with us, silver is a legal tender, although it is not a tender, but as small change, in England. If we can so regulate the value of our paper money as to make it equal to silver in the purchase of foreign exchange, then all that we have to do is to so regulate the price of all other commodities that their price, if sold for our paper money, will command the same amount of foreign exchange as if they were sold for silver or gold. If the price of gold be twice the value of our paper, then our cotton should bring twice the price in our paper money as if sold for gold. If we make the paper money a tender, and regulate the quantity, in circulation, by a proper system of taxing and funding it, we can make it of equal value as gold in the payment of debts and the purchase of property, including foreign exchange.

SUCH PAPER MONEY WILL BE WORTH MORE THAN SPECIE, as I now proceed to demonstrate. By the report of the Secretary of the Treasury of the United States, there were in the banks in the non slaveholding States, in 1860, $44,662,408 of specie, and in the banks of the slaveholding States, $38,912,129. This sum was held by the banks to enable them to redeem their circulation, which, in the Northern States, was $119,997,469, and in the slaveholding States, $87,107,108. It paid no interest, and, to use the words of Adam Smith, was so much dead capital. What the sum held by individuals was, I have no sufficient *data* to state, except that the coinage in the United States, from 1850 to 1856 inclusive, adding six months of 1857, was $415,226,717.74, of which there were exported $285,881,176, leaving $129,345,541.74. Now, if we assume that the interest, upon the specie held by the banks and the public in the Confederate States, is but ten millions ($10,000,000) per annum, and that that sum was substituted, by the public and the banks, by the six per cent. convertible bonds, as I propose, the saving to the banks and to the public, holding specie, would, in forty years, be $1,660,285,359.$\frac{62}{100}$; and yet, great as this saving would be, it is, as it were, small, very small indeed, as compared to the effect which the increased stimulus given to the productive industry of the country would be, and to the saving in the expenditures and taxes of the Government of the Confederacy and of the several States. The States cannot make their Treasury Notes a legal tender, but they can issue their certificates, fundable in six per cent. convertible bonds, and authorize the suspension of *specie* payments by their banks, if the holders of bank notes refuse to receive the fundable certificates of the State or of the Confederate States in payment, upon condition that the banks have deposited, with the Treasurer of the State, the convertible bonds of the State or of the Confederate States, to be held in trust for the payment of their notes. In such case, the holders of the notes will know that the banks cannot fail; and, unless the value of the money be less than the interest paid upon the bonds, the notes will not be presented for payment, and the value of the currency will be as uniform as the rate of interest paid upon the bonds. As there will be no apprehension of their failure, there will be no inducement to run upon the banks; and, as money would be abundant and cheap, the greater part of the surplus capital of the whole country would be invested in public securities or in banks, whose profits would consist chiefly in the circulation of their own notes. And, as under such a system, there would be no sudden or ruinous contraction of the currency—no sudden or ruinous depreciation of the values of property, it would be the business of our banks to stimulate the energies, industry and enterprise of our people, by an advance of the requisite capital, whenever the previous habits and character of the applicant, sustained by the requisite security, would justify it. This is not theory. The principle has been fully tested in Scotland. I refer to the comment of the London *Quarterly Review* for March, 1830, upon the Report of the select committee on promissory notes in Scotland and Ireland in 1826, and give the following extracts upon

### SCOTCH BANKING.

If, however, the privilege of issuing negociable notes was granted to banks only on terms which would remove all doubt from the public mind as to the solvency of these establishments, a run never would practically take place. The holders of these notes, knowing that they ran no possible risk of loss, would be no more disposed to rush with them into the different banks, to be converted into cash, than to run with a sovereign into the mint to have it exchanged for bullion. The cause of every run upon banking establishments is the fear which, from whatever unforeseen cause, seizes the public mind that they may not be solvent. Let the ground of this fear be effectually removed; assure the public mind that, as far, at least, as concerns the notes circulated by a banking establishment, it cannot prove insolvent, and these runs will never take place.

That a system of banking might be organized in this country, (England), which would practically remove every danger and inconvenience attendant upon the issue of one pound notes, is a fact capable of being demonstrated by the evidence of actual experience. It has already been put to the test in one part of His Majesty's dominions, and has been found to stand its ground, unaffected by the violent and sudden fluctuations which, at various periods, have taken place in the transactions of trade and commerce. We need not tell our readers that we allude to Scotland, where the circulating medium (with the exception of silver for change) consists wholly of paper, and where a sovereign, as a current coin, is rarely ever seen. But, although it be well known that paper money forms the whole circulating medium of Scotland, we are inclined to suspect that the principles of the banking system of our Northern neighbors are not generally understood, or, at least, generally appreciated in this part of the empire. Nothing but the want of adequate information, as to this subject, could have led to the attempt which was made, in 1826, to meddle with the banking system of Scotland, and deprive the inhabitants of that country of institutions, under the protection of which they had reached, and continued to enjoy, a high degree of public as well as private prosperity. Our wary neighbors, however, led on by the redoubted Malagrowther (Sir Walter Scott), successfully resisted the attempts of the Treasury to force upon them the use of a metallic circulating medium, and, by that means, secured themselves (in as far as the intimate connexion of the two countries could permit) against the difficulties and inconveniences which the change, effected at that period, in our monetary system, has entailed upon this part of the Island. An impression prevails very generally, on this side of the Tweed, that the superior stability of the Scottish Banking system rests upon the proverbial sagacity and wariness of the inhabitants of Scotland, and not upon any peculiarity inherent in the system itself. From this it is inferred that a circulating medium, which has been found safe among our Northern neighbors, would be attended with danger and insecurity, if adopted here. This, however, appears to us a mistake. The security of Scottish banking arises from the general principles on which the system has been organized, and not from anything which is peculiar either to the character or the habits of those by whom its operations are conducted. If adopted elsewhere, these principles would, we feel persuaded, be attended with similar results: hence it becomes important to point out their nature and trace their effects.

\* \* Even in times of commercial panic and confusion, the inhabitants of Scotland never, for a single moment, harbor the suspicion that their principal banks can, by possibility, fail. \* \* \* The principles on which the banks are established place their solvency beyond all doubt. All the banks which issue notes are joint stock companies, consisting of a great number of partners, and, possessing a large capital, not merely subscribed, but actually paid up, and invested in mortgages or in Government securities. This fund is always ready to cover any losses which the bank may sustain in its transactions. * * * * * * This is in truth the foundation of the unlimited credit enjoyed by the Scotch banks; it is the basis of that undoubting confidence which the public repose in their stability. The public confidence does not rest upon the credit, the discretion or the integrity of the directors; it has a much more stable foundation for its support; it is based upon actual capital which can neither be withdrawn nor diminished *without the knowledge of the public.*

In that country, as we have said, a sovereign is seldom seen, except in the card case of an old maid, or the cabinet of some recluse virtuoso. One of the witnesses says: "There is a prejudice against gold in Scotland. This prejudice is simply on account of the trouble attending it: it is weighed; when it is found light, the people refuse it; the country people are afraid to touch it. There is not a district in Scotland but where, if you were endeavoring to pass a sovereign, they would say, if you had a note of any bank in Scotland they would prefer it.

There is, no doubt, a small quantity of gold in the coffers of the different bankers, in order to meet the occasional whim of some capricious customer; but that a bank should be asked to give gold in exchange for notes is an event which happens so rarely, that a very trifling sum, indeed, is found fully adequate to meet all demands of this kind.

"Although," says a witness, examined before the committee, "I have been for ten years in an office that, perhaps, does more business than any other individual office in Scotland, or out of London, I can state, as my experience, that I have never refused gold to any person that wished it. They only ask it when they have occasion to go to Ireland or to England, or to emigrate to America. I could state it as a fact that ten thousand sovereigns would have supplied all the demands for the ten years I have been in Glasgow." "The rottenness and insecurity of the English system of banking are known to aggravate very greatly the effects of the panics to which all bodies, trading upon credit, are unavoidably subject. The general distrust prevailing at such periods is particularly directed toward the English banks, which are sure to be the first to feel the raging of the storm. The weakest of these fail, and this adds fuel to the flame which had already burst forth. A partial want of confidence is thus speedily converted into a general panic, and all banks, whatever may be their opulence and character, suffer more or less from the consequences. Even banks, upon which no actual run takes place, sustain great losses during these seasons. Uncertain of the direction which the tempest may take, they are all compelled to make preparations to meet its violence, and the sacrifice of property required for this purpose has frequently been enormous. The faintest whisper or the most trifling accident, often proves sufficient to inflict incalculable losses on English Banks. * * * * * The bankers of Scotland do not, like those of England, derive their profits from the employment of floating balances left in their hands without interest by those who deal with them. On the contrary, they allow interest for every pound of capital deposited in their hand; this interest is always less by one per cent. than that which they charge upon the loans advanced to borrowers; and the difference between the interest paid and that charged upon the whole of the capital entrusted to their management, forms the only source whence the profits of Scotch banking accrue."

"By this practice, allowing interest upon all deposits, these banks attract every shilling of unemployed capital which any inhabitant may happen to possess. The witnesses, who were examined by the committee of 1826, estimated the average of these deposits at about twenty millions sterling. Persons possessed of small capitals in Scotland never purchase into the public funds; having the most unbounded confidence in the solidity of their own banks, they universally deposit in these establishments all the capital which they can spare * * * * Their general rule is to allow interest upon every deposit, however small may be its amount. One of the witnesses examined by the committee, and thoroughly conversant with the subject, states that, in towns like Glasgow, a very large proportion of the deposits come from the laboring classes. In country places, like Perth or Aberdeen, it is from servants and fishermen, and just the class of the community who save from their earnings, in mere trifles, small sums, till they reach a sufficient amount to form a bank deposit. * * * A great part of the depositors are of this description."

Another witness examined touching the same point, estimates the whole bank deposits at twenty millions sterling ($100,000,000), and the proportion of the small deposits as fully equal to one-half the whole. He then adds: "I have had many opportunities, both professionally and in various situations in which I have been placed, of observing the effects of those deposits; and I do think that the system of the Scotch banks, allowing the rates of interest which they have done, upon these small deposits, has influenced very considerably the moral character of the people. The deposit is seldom drawn out until the depositor has to build a cottage or to buy a house; or perhaps he himself begin business, or set out his eldest son in the world; or, it may be, furnish a house for his daughter at her marriage. A deposit is often laid up for old age; and, in many instances, I have no doubt, has likewise been the means of enabling men in the humble class of society to give their children what we in Scotland value above all the advantages of wealth—the benefit of an intellectual and religious education."

"In truth, nothing can be conceived more admirably adapted to encourage industry and economy than the system of banking which has been so long in full operation in Scotland; and we have no doubt that the saving and persevering disposition, which forms a prominent feature in the character of our Northern neighbors, must be ascribed, in a considerable degree, to the habits instilled into them by these valuable institutions. The industrious laborer finds, at his own door, a safe and profitable receptacle for every shilling he can save. Without trouble, anxiety, or loss of time, he takes his pound to the bank, where it bears interest from the moment in which it is deposited. The banks thus constitute public depositories, in which every shilling that can be spared, throughout every district of Scotland, finds its place." "Nor is the disposal of the aggregate capital thus collected less beneficial in its effects, upon the habits and enterprise of the people, than the economy by which it is saved. The bank reservoirs, thus kept constantly full, furnish every person of character and enterprise with a ready, certain, and never failing supply of capital, wherewith to embark in any undertaking which holds out the reasonable probability of success. The managers of the different banks, having collected into one focus the whole capital of the country, offer every facility to those who wish to borrow this capital, and turn it to profitable account. Their profit is derived exclusively from this source. Upon all the capital which may be unemployed in the coffers of these banks a dead loss is sustained: hence they are eager to find out safe borrowers as saving depositors."

The bankers of Scotland are, in fact, dealers in unemployed capital. They form an open and universally known channel of communication between the borrower and the lender in the money market. They acquire a perfect knowledge of both parties. They borrow money of those who have it to lend, and lend money to those who want to borrow, and charge a profit of one per cent. upon all cash transactions for the use of their own credit, labor and skill. Any person, opening an account with the Scotch banks, receives four per cent. (or some other amount less by one per cent. than the average rate of interest) upon the balance left in their hands. He may pay in money whatever he chooses. This is carried to the credit of his account, and interest is allowed for it from the day on which it is deposited. He may draw his money out when and in what sums he thinks proper, and his loss of interest on the sums so drawn out commences only from the day on which it is received. Their object, however, in borrowing capital, is to make a profit by lending it: hence the facilities which they give to borrowers are as great as they can be consistently with safety. In the first place, they will discount bills and other mercantile securities, which are perfectly regular and good, at all times and to any amount. This is an incalculable advantage to the merchants of Scotland. They know that they can fail of success only through their own rashness or miscalculation—never from any sudden withdrawal of that accommodation which had originally stimulated their enterprise. The inconvenience felt by the merchants of Scotland, during times of panic, arise exclusively from their transactions with England, where the storm, whenever it happens, rages with destructive violence.

A second mode of lending, practiced by the Scotch bankers, is to grant what is called a *cash credit* to any industrious person desirous to borrow capital, to be embarked in any species of profitable employment. When a person applies for a cash account, which is not an immediate advance of money on the part of the bank, but a conferring of the power of drawing upon the bank for a certain specified extent, he proposes two or more securities; a bond is made out, and he draws as occasion requires. In this way he has never more from the bank than is absolutely necessary for the purposes of his business. The account is never recalled unless, by having been but little operated upon, it has ceased to be beneficial to the banker in the circulation of his notes; and interest is charged only on the amount of the balance which may be owing to the bank. These credits run from so low as £50 to £1000, and in some instances more. They are granted to persons of every description—to small farmers, who require assistance in stocking their farms, or who carry on a petty trade in cattle; to shop keepers, principally on their commencing business; to tradesmen generally; to all sorts of law agents. The beneficial effects of this system are incalculable with regard both to the interests of individuals and the public. * * * * It is on all hands agreed that, for the rapid advances which it has for the last century made in wealth and prosperity, Scotland is very largely, if not mainly, indebted to her banking system.

I regret that want of space compels me to limit my extracts relative to Scotch banks, for the system has become so identified with the progress, the industry, the commerce and civilization of mankind, that, in considering the question of currency, we should remember that banks and bankers have become an indispensable part of the system of credits—that it is their business to deal in money and in credit, and that, therefore, they are an important agency in the regulation of the value of money. Hence the necessity of a careful examination into the history and nature of banks and banking, that we may guard against the defects of existing systems and the errors which have characterised their administration. Thus we see that in Scotland and New York banking is free, yet the amount of circulation is comparatively less than in England and some of the other States where it is limited by severe penalties and restrictions. We see, also, that, under the Scotch system, the accommodation given to the public is much greater than in England; and yet, in the midst of failures and bankruptcies which have characterised the British system, during the panic of 1826, when more than four hundred banks failed in England, there was not a single failure in Scotland.

I have referred to the organization of the Bank of the United States, and of the agency of that bank in depleting the other banks of specie, to be remitted to London preparatory of the resumption of specie payment

by the Bank of England. As the ultimate failure of the Bank of the United States was the result of political and financial combinations, a proper explanation of which would, as I believe, furnish forcible arguments in support of the measures I propose, I very briefly refer to them.
* It is known that Mr. Clay and John Q. Adams were American commissioners at Ghent, and that the tenth article of the treaty of peace bound the United States to co operate with England in preventing the trade in African slaves, which was construed by Mr. Adams to include the domestic as well as the foreign slave trade. From Ghent Mr. Adams went to London as the American Minister, where he was in contact with the leading British Abolitionists. In 1816, Mr. Monroe appointed Mr. Cook, of Illinois, bearer of dispatches notifying Mr. Adams of his appointment as Secretary of State. I then resided in Kentucky. Mr. Cook brought a letter of introduction, and told me that, being in delicate health, his purpose, in going to Europe, was to try the effect of a sea voyage, intending, on his return, to remove to the South. I saw him the next year in Washington, when he told me that Mr. Adams had satisfied him that the migration to the north of the Ohio would be such that the anti slavery party would soon control the political destiny of the United States, and that, under the advice of Mr. Adams, instead of going South to live, he was going back to Illinois with a view to come into Congress and agitate the slavery question. He said that he had already commenced the agitation, and gave me a pamphlet, containing a series of letters, written by him, addressed to Mr. Monroe, under the signature of D. P. C., which had been published in Meade's Register, and contained the text of the slavery agitation in Congress and in the press from the time of the Missouri Question until now. He did go to Illinois, was elected to Congress, and took a leading part in enacting the Missouri restriction. I removed to Missouri in 1817. John Scott was our delegate in Congress. I was in the army of 1812. I was sick at Vincennes, where his mother nursed me as if I had been her son. I did not forget her kindness, and was the intimate, personal and political friend of her son. Peculiar circumstances gave me a controlling influence in the Western part of the State. I was a member of the Convention which adopted the State Constitution, and then of the House of Representatives and of the Senate. Col. Benton, having been driven from Tennessee by General Jackson, went to St. Louis and established the St. Louis *Enquirer*. Being, constitutionally, a parasite, he attached himself to Governor Clarke. I had been a classmate at school of George Croghan and John O. Fallon, the Governor's nephews, and was received by him with special favor, and was his devoted personal and political friend. Party politics were there, as in most new countries, chiefly personal. In the distribution of offices, under the State Government, Mr. Scott was elected to the House of Representatives and Benton to the Senate. In 1823, Benton, then a partisan of Mr. Clay, came to St. Charles, where the Legislature was in session, and urged a caucus nomination of Mr. Clay for the Presidency. I opposed the nomination, and it was rejected by a nearly unanimous vote. I, immediately after this, purchased the St. Louis *Enquirer* and removed to St. Louis, and took an active part in support of the election of General Jackson. Col. Benton returned to Missouri from Washington, and can-

vassed the State actively for Mr. Clay. Wherever he went in the State, he found the influence of my paper counteracting his efforts. The vote of the Southern District was cast for the Jackson elector; the other two were given in favor of Mr. Clay by a small majority. Mr. Clay's half brother happened to be the returning officer in one of the Southern counties, and refused to make returns. Mr. Clay's partisans had taken the ground, in a circular issued by his Kentucky committee, of which John J. Crittenden was a member, that if the election devolved upon the House, it would there be carried by "bargain, intrigue and management;" and yet, they urged that, as Mr. Clay was popular in Congress, if returned as one of three, he would be elected.

The Legislature, acting under the advice of Col. Benton, declared the election of electors illegal, and gave to Mr. Clay the three electoral votes of Missouri, hoping to secure his election by Congress. Jackson, Adams and Crawford, to the exclusion of Mr. Clay, were returned to the House of Representatives, and Mr. Adams was elected by the votes of Mr. Clay, Mr. Scott, of Missouri, and Mr. Cook, of Illinois.

It so happened that, as the attorney for persons having large claims against the Government, I reached Washington a few days after the election of Mr. Adams. One of my family relatives and J. Q. Adams had married sisters. Mr. Cook had married my niece; and inasmuch as Mr. Clay had been assailed for his vote for Mr. Adams, it was deemed important to secure the influence of my paper in his support, and my nephew, Mr. Cook, and my friend, Mr. Scott, were selected to make the arrangement—Col. Benton having availed himself of the election of Mr. Adams to go over to the support of General Jackson as a means of identifying himself with the party which I had organized in the State. They rolled up the curtain of their future; they tendered me the support of the Government as a candidate for the United States Senate, in opposition to Mr. Benton, with a controlling influence over the Federal patronage in the State.

I saw that the purpose of the coalition was to create a sectional party in the North, for the purpose of governing and controlling the Union. Mr. Adams, relying upon the anti-slavery element, and Mr. Clay, standing astride of the Alleghanies, with one foot on a high tariff to enrich the Yankee manufacturers, and the other upon turnpike roads for the benefit of the Northwest, I saw that the sinking fund of ten millions of dollars then appropriated to that object would, in a few years, discharge the national debt; and that, instead of a system which would increase the public revenue, creating a large surplus to be expended under appropriations to be made by a corrupt sectional majority in Congress, it was indispensable to so modify the tariff as to reduce the current revenue to the proper expenditures of the Government. Instead of supporting the coalition, I purchased the *Telegraph*, and removed to Washington to oppose them.

General Jackson was elected. I had made an arrangement with Amos Kendal to remove to Washington and aid me as an associate editor. I had been a schoolmate of T. P. Moore, of Kentucky. He had been my active friend, and had gained the *soubriquet* of "*Free Tom*" by aiding in the circulation of my paper. After Gen. Jackson had reached Washington, Moore requested me to aid in obtaining for him the appointment of Postmaster General. I refused to do so. A few days afterward, Col. Richard M. Johnson told me that the partisans of Martin Van Buren had, after consultation, determined to put him in nomination for the Presidency in 1832; that the selection of the Cabinet and the important foreign missions had been arranged with a view to aid his election; and that, in that consultation, Moore had told them that he had known me from a boy, and that they could not control me or my press through the public patronage; and advised that, instead of permitting Kendal to be my associate editor, they should make him an Auditor, with the understanding that he would establish a Van Buren paper when it became necessary.

When Major Lewis brought me the names of the Cabinet, upon reading them, I went to General Jackson and told him what I had heard from Col. Johnson, and said to him that I was yet a young man—that I had made some reputation as an editor—that I was then the Printer to both Houses of Congress—that my paper had, as I believed, a greater circulation than any other political paper in the United States—that I had one of the best, if not the most valuable, printing offices in the United States—that I could not and would not support Mr. Van Buren for the Presidency—that I was unwilling to come in conflict with my political friends—that I was young enough to return to my profession—that I wanted no office in his gift, but if his purpose was as I had been told, then it was my wish that he would select some one else, who could purchase my paper—that I asked no advance upon the actual cost, and no compensation for my services in the past. My objection to Mr. Van Buren was, that I believed that as soon as he believed that, by the influence of the party organization, aided by the public patronage, he could command the Southern vote, he would then bid against Mr. Clay and Mr. Adams for the Northern vote, and thus strengthen that sectional organization which it was my desire to defeat.

General Jackson urged me to remain, pledging himself, in the most solemn manner possible, that if any member of his Cabinet should, at any time, use the patronage of his department with a view to promote the election of Mr. Van Buren, the member doing so should resign; and, as an earnest of his sincerity, said that the first official act, after his inauguration, would be to cause the patronage of the State department to be sent to my office, which he did. I have not the time or space, now, to explain the measures or the motives which, if General Jackson was sincere in the pledges then given, induced him afterward to exert his whole personal and official influence in aid of the election of Mr. Van Buren as his successor, although it is my purpose, if life and health permit, to do so hereafter. I recur to them now to explain that the purpose of Mr. Adams and Mr. Clay being to organize a sectional Northern party, predicated on the emancipation of our slaves, and a system of high duties for the benefit of Northern manufacturers for making turnpike roads, to be constructed under the patronage of a corrupt sectional Northern Congressional majority for the purpose of electing Mr. Clay President, and Gen. Jackson having become the acknowledged partisan of Mr. Van Buren, the near approach of the payment of the national debt, whilst admitting the full power of Congress to lay and collect duties requisite to pay the debts and carry on the Government, had made it necessary for those who did not believe that they had the power to increase the duties for the purpose of creating a large surplus revenue, to be expended under appropriations made by a corrupt sectional majority of Congress, to rally all their energies and resources to prevent a system of measures which we foresaw, and foretold must result in sectional conflicts which would, of necessity, alienate the South from the North, and, if not arrested, terminate in a dissolution of the Union. Hence the nullification of South Carolina was a movement for the preservation of the Union by restraining the action of Congress within the powers granted by the Constitution. That movement was, for a time, successful. The subsequent action of Van Buren fully justified my opposition to him, and the crisis in which we are now placed proves not only the propriety, but the necessity, os the measures which I have again and again urged upon the people of the slaveholding States. How different would have been our present position if, as a people, the South had adopted, with proper energy, the system of measures which I have recommended. One purpose of this statement is to show that the opposition to the tariff of 1828, and to Mr. Clay's American system, was not, as many believe, an opposition to domestic manufactures. It was an opposition to the organization of a sectional party upon principles and measures in open violation of the letter and spirit of the Constitution, which, it was foreseen, must terminate in the dissolution of the Union.

Another purpose is to refer to the fact that Congress being driven, by the action of South Carolina and of the State Rights party, to modify the tariff of 1828, and the payment of the public debt having left a large surplus of public funds in the Bank of the United States, Van Buren induced General Jackson to go through Pennsylvania and New York to Boston, where he was met by Mr. Van Buren and several of his leading political partizans, who, Mr. Poinsett dissenting, as he assured me he did, induced him to seize upon the public deposits, which were transferred from the Bank, where they were placed by operation of law, and placed on deposit in local Banks, selected by a partisan Secretary of the Treasury. It was the influence of the public money in these banks, and the corrupt abuse of the public patronage which elected Mr. Van Buren. This transfer of the public deposits to the pet banks led to a vast expansion of the currency, and immense speculations, especially in the public lands, so that, although the average sales for the ten years preceding General Jackson's election, did not amount to 800,000 acres, 12,564,218 acres were sold in 1835, and 20,074,870 acres were sold in 1836; and although there were, in 1830, but 330 banks, with a circulation of $61,323,898, there were 634 banks, with a circulation of $149,185,890, in 1837.*

\* NOTE.—The following table shows the number of banks that were in the United States, their capital, loans and discounts, specie, circulation, and deposits, from 1830 to 1840 inclusive:

| Date. | No. of Banks. | Capital. | Loans and Discounts. | Specie. | Circulation. | Deposits. |
|---|---|---|---|---|---|---|
| Jan. 1820 | 308 | $137,110,611 | | $19,820,240 | $ 44,863,344 | $ 35,950,470 |
| " 1830 | 330 | 145,192,268 | $200,451,214 | 22,114,917 | 61,323,898 | 55,559,828 |
| " 1834 | 500 | 200,005,944 | 324,119,499 | | 94,839,570 | 75,666,986 |
| " 1835 | 558 | 231,250,337 | 365,163,834 | 43,937,625 | 103,692,495 | 83,081,365 |
| " 1836 | 567 | 251,875,292 | 457,506,080 | 40,019,594 | 140,301,038 | 115,104,444 |
| " 1837 | 634 | 290,772,041 | 525,115,702 | 37,915,340 | 149,185,890 | 127,397,185 |
| " 1838 | 663 | 317,636,778 | 485,631,687 | 35,184,112 | 116,138,910 | 84,691,184 |
| " 1839 | 662 | 327,132,512 | 492,278,015 | 45,132,673 | 135,170,995 | 90,240,146 |
| " 1840 | 722 | 358,442,692 | 462,896,523 | 33,105,155 | 106,968,572 | 75,696,857 |

speculations and this expansion of the currency took place cotempo-
ly with like speculations and expansion of the currency in England
ent upon the placing, by the Government, in the Bank of England, of
e sums, paid under the acts emancipating the West India slaves and
ogation of the East India monopoly, being about $120,000,000, the
part of which; in anticipation of the payments, to be made by the
as loaned to money dealers, and the consequence was an inflation of
ency nearly or quite as great as in the United States. The payment
Bank of England to the proper claimants, as their accounts were ad-
nd, the transfer from the pet banks of the surplus revenues to the States
n act of Congress, operating in England and the United States at the
ne, caused the reaction in both countries, inflicting unexampled pecuniary
nd distress, originating in both countries from the efforts of those who
e control of the currency to increase their power and influence by
e of a defective system of finance. Had England made her
i the shape of certificates receivable in public dues and fundable, as I
, a legal tender, the excess would have been funded, and there would
en no inflation of the currency, and consequently no reactionary de-
or specie, and no pecuniary losses or bankruptcy. Had the United
ssued their credit in the form and fundable as proposed, there would
en no surplus revenue in the banks, no speculation in the public lands,
e circular, issued by a party President to protect the pet banks from
rand for specie, the consequence of the over-issue of their circulation
f the corrupt speculations of political favorites.
pretence for the transfer of the public deposits from the Bank of the
States to the pet banks was, that the power of that bank would be
and hence the pet banks were required, by an order from the Secre-

llowing table shows the number of acres of public land offered for sale, the acres
amount paid by purchasers, and the average price paid per acre for the several
ren:

| Acres offered for sale. | Acres Sold. | Amount paid by purchasers. | Average price. |
|---|---|---|---|
| 7,294,186 | 749,323 | $ 953,799 | $ 1.27 |
| 3,418,604 | 893,461 | 1,205,068 | 1.35 |
| 2,880,703 | 848,082 | 1,128,617 | 1.33 |
| 3,314,816 | 926,727 | 1,318,305 | 1.42 |
| 3,268,493 | 965,600 | 1,221,357 | 1.26 |
| 6,149,962 | 1,244,860 | 1,572,863 | 1.26 |
| 6,750,798 | 1,929,733 | 2,433,432 | 1.26 |
| 11,005,561 | 2,777,856 | 3,557,023 | 1.28 |
| 4,205,805 | 2,462,342 | 3,115,376 | 1.27 |
| 6,614,596 | 3,856,227 | 4,972,284 | 1.29 |
| 13,056,865 | 4,658,218 | 6,099,881 | 1.31 |
| 13,767,268 | 12,564,478 | 15,999,804 | 1.27 |
| 509,034 | 20,074,870 | 25,167,833 | 1.25 |
| . . . . . | 4,805,162 | 6,127,418 | 1.28 |
| 122,512,384 | 61,296,411 | $78,340,557 | $1 27¾ |

tary of the Treasury, to discount freely, and thus prevent the monetary crisis which, by some it was urged, would be the consequence of the sudden withdrawal of so large a deposit. Failing to get a renewal of its charter from Congress, the bank obtained a charter from the Legislature of Pennsylvania, and instead of reducing their line of discounts, the Directory availed themselves of the inflation of the currency to sell out their branches, receiving the notes of the pet banks in payment; and, instead of making war upon the pet banks by demanding payment in specie, the large sums thus obtained were invested in public securities and in advances upon cotton, intending, by the sale of the cotton and the State securities in Europe, to reinstate the capital which had been invested in the branches; and Biddle and Humphries were sent to Liverpool as the agents of the bank charged with the sale of the cotton, and Mr. Jaudon, the cashier, was sent to London with the State' securities. The great fire in New York had deprived many of the merchants of that city of the means of paying the large sums falling due to their British creditors. The bank, under the advice of Mr. Biddle, relying on the sale of cotton by Biddle and Iumphries, and of State securities by Mr. Jaudon, advanced large sums in the shape of bills on London and Paris. Before this time, any American merchant who could get an acceptance by Wilde, Wiggin or Wilsons, three American houses in London, could purchase British goods upon six and twelve months credit. Apprehending a monetary crisis, Wiggin wrote to his American correspondents that he could no longer accept as he had done. His having done so came to the knowledge of the Directors of the Bank of England. The Governor of that bank called on Mr. Wiggin and urged him to withdraw his letters, saying that the English warehouses were filled with goods; and, as the bank wished to encourage the trade with America, although he could not pledge the bank, yet as governor of the bank, he would exert his influence to sustain Mr. Wiggin in case of a crisis. Under that pledge Mr. Wiggin recalled his letters, and was under acceptance for more than thirteen millions of dollars, when the bank passed an order that no bill, predicated on any transactions in American produce, should be discounted in bank. The consequence was that Wilde, Wiggin and Wilsons all failed - that Biddle and Iumphries could not sell cotton, nor could Jaudon sell the securities upon which he relied to protect the credit of the Bank of the United States, and he was compelled to make hypothecations and borrow money at rates which was followed by so great a depreciation of the values of the securities, in which the capital of the bank was invested, as ultimately to absorb much the greater part of its assets.

I do not charge that the conduct of the Bank of England was purposely intended to inflict the severe suffering and distress which were its consequence; nor do 1 charge that the assurances of aid, given by the Governor of the Bank to Mr. Wiggin, were intended to induce him to make acceptances which he (the Governor) knew he would not be able to meet. But I do charge that the fluctuations in the value of money and property were the inevitable resulting consequence of the system of currency and finance which compelled the Bank, to use the words of Samuel Jones Lloyd, to "SAVE HERSELF BY THE DESTRUCTION OF ALL AROUND HER." Thus, if we recur to the crisis of 1794, we find the directory of the Bank in a formal protest to the Government, notifying the Minister "*that if any further loan* or advance of money to the Emperor, or to any of the foreign States, should, in the present state of affairs, take place, *it will in all probability prove fatal to the Bank of England.* It was indispensably necessary to make the loan, and hence the Bank, in 1797, was forced to suspend specie payment. Again, in 1814 and 1815, the loans to the allies of England were $96,831,539, and there was unexampled distress. Again, in the eight years, from 1818 to 1825 inclusive, the sums advanced on foreign loans and speculative schemes was $522,692,500, and the consequence was, that the demand for specie was so severe and the depreciation of the value of property so great, as to cause unparalleled loss, bankruptcy and distress. Again, in 1836-37, the Government having placed in the Bank of England the funds intended to pay the West India claimants, large sums were loaned to the money dealers—this gave birth to speculations, the currency was increased, prices were consequently inflated, to be followed by a reaction, causing, if possible, still greater reduction of prices, with greater pecuniary losses and distress. And again, in 1853 to 1857, the demand for gold to pay the expenses of the wars in the Crimea, in India and China, created a renewed demand for gold and silver, acting upon the values of property precisely in the same manner. Now, why did these frequent recurring demands for money always cause a ruinous depreciation in the values of property, enriching the creditor without merit and impoverishing the debtor without fault? Was it not because the creditor was enabled to compel the debtor to make payment in gold, under the delusion that gold and silver are more uniform and stable in value than any other medium of purchase or payment, and that therefore nothing but gold and silver should be recognized as money?

Is it necessary to adduce additional facts or arguments to prove that this is a delusion? We have seen that the average specie in the banks of the city of New York, from 1853 to October, 1857, was about eleven and a half millions, whilst the daily average settlements between the banks alone were about thirty millions of dollars, and the daily average settlements between individuals, which do not appear in the returns of the Clearing House, are estimated at fifty millions of dollars, and Colwell estimates the payments made through the banks in the United States in 1857, by set off, without one dollar in specie, at *eighty-five thousand millions of dollars,* and we are told by Chivalier, that the amount of the Bills of Exchange, at one time in circulation in Great Britain, was £180,000,000, or $900,000,000.

These facts prove that property, and not specie, is the true basis of credit, and that a currency predicated on the entire property of an agricultural and commercial country, may be made much more uniform and stable in value than if convertible into gold, for surely it will not be necessary to adduce other proofs to demonstrate that every monetary crisis, every general suspension of the banks in the United States, has been caused by the monetary revulsions which have occurred in England, and the demand for specie created through the Bank of England. My proposition is to create for the Confederate States a currency predicated on the entire property of the whole country. The value of be regulated by receiving nothing but the public credit or gold in payment of taxes, and to cause the excess, if any there be, to be funded in convertible bonds bearing a proper rate of interest. Thus say that the current expenditures after peace, including the interest on the public debt, will be one hundred millions of dollars, and that the annual taxes be the same, it will require the whole sum of the current issue to pay the taxes, and any deficiency must be paid in gold, or by reconverting so much of the funded debt as may be requisite. If the banks are required to redeem their notes in the Confederate currency, and to place the convertible funded debt with the Treasurers of the several States, in trust for that purpose, then the value of the Treasury Certificates will be regulated by the rate of interest paid upon the funded debt, and the value of the bank notes will be regulated by the value of the certificates.

God, in His Providence, has given to the people of the Confederate States sources of individual independence, wealth and prosperity, such as He has given to no other people on the globe. He has given us a soil and climate peculiarly adapted to the cultivation of cotton and wool; He has filled our mountains with a greater abundance of mineral wealth; He has given us an abundant supply of living streams, which, in their progress from our mountains to the sea, proclaim in a language not to be misunderstood the purpose of their creation ; He has given us a territory so large and so fertile, as to be capable of feeding a population as great as that of Europe ; He has given us the labor peculiarly adapted to the cultivation of the great staples which constitute the chief elements of modern industry and of modern commerce. He has so identified the interests of the governing class with those of the servile race, as to secure to us a purer religion, a more refined individual and social morality, and a more enlightened, more independent, and a freer political organization than He has given to any other nation upon earth. He has separated us from the rest of mankind, as He separated His chosen people under the Mosaic dispensation, and that He has had a special purpose in doing so, no one, who carefully and prayerfully studies the manifestations of His will and the indication of His purposes, can doubt. He has not so richly endowed us, as a people, by accident. His purpose is forcibly illustrated by the parable given in the twenty-fifth chapter of Matthew—we are but trustees, and are responsible to God for the manner in which we execute the trust committed to us. If we would discharge our duty, we must so use the abundance which we possess as best to promote His purpose and glory, and this cannot be done unless we become a manufacturing and commercial, as well as an agricultural people; and this we cannot do unless we so organize our credit as to make it available in the development of our abundant resources, and enable us successfully to compete with the most favored nations in all the mechanic arts, the manufactures, and the commerce, which characterize the progress of modern society.

The measures which I propose will simplify the functions of the Confederate Government. It will reduce the action of that Government to the payment of the current expenses, and collecting the current taxes after funding the existing debt. It will greatly curtail the corrupting influence of Executive patronage. It will give greater stability to the values of the currency, and consequently to the values of property, and it will give us an abundant and cheap currency, uniform and stable in value, giving life and energy to the productive industry of the country in all the departments of labor. It will lessen the burden of taxation by substituting the certificates of the Confederate and State Governments for bank notes convertible into specie, and save to the Government, and to the public, and to the banks, the interest on the mass of specie which, under a revival of a specie currency, must be held as the basis of credit. It will enable us to organize a system of education, embracing the children of our deceased soldiers, enabling all females as well as males, to earn the compensation requisite to feed, clothe and educate themselves, training them to be useful members of society, self-reliant, and self-sustaining, inspiring the rising generation with a proper sense of personal independence and of public liberty.

The experience of the war demonstrates the necessity of a greater distribution of labor, and to do this requires an appropriation of the requisite capital in aid of the efforts of individual enterprise. There is a praiseworthy movement to organize an ample fund to educate the children of our deceased soldiers. I would embrace all of the rising generation—the children of the living and of the dead—the rich and the poor; and would so diversify their training and their knowledge as to enable them to relieve us from our dependence upon the foreign markets for articles which may be better and cheaper produced at home. The public debt in the shape of convertible interest bearing bonds, deposited with the Treasurers of the several States, as the basis of bank issues, will give us an abundant, cheap and stable currency, and banks organized for the purpose of advancing requisite capital to competent persons who will employ male and females in appropriate departments of labor, with the understanding that their compensation shall be such that six, or at most eight, hours labor per day shall be sufficient to pay for their clothing, board and tuition, and also to provide a surplus fund to aid them in the outset of life, will give to the shareholders of such banks a proper profit on the capital thus invested, and stimulate the energies and industry of the employer, giving to the children from four to six hours for study, with twelve hours per day for refreshment and recreation.

Such a system can be organized if the Government will make the Treasury certificates a tender, and adopt the system of finance and currency which I propose. It will convert the public debt into a fund; will build our railroads, establish our manufactures, and educate our children, and make us the most enlightened and prosperous people upon the face of the globe. It will do more. It will achieve our financial independence by elevating us above the controlling influence of that new power in Europe, so forcibly described in the article from the London *Spectator*, given in the appendix, which will then be no longer able to place us beneath the pressure of the machinery by which they regulate the value of the property of all those who are subject to its control.

THE EFFECT OF FUNDING AT A LOW RATE OF INTEREST is forcibly illustrated by the history of the public debt of England and the system of finance under which that debt was created. It would seem that our Congress and the late Secretary of the Treasury believe that the excellence of human wisdom consists in tracing, as nearly as possible, the example of England. Thus, instead of giving value to our currency by funding the surplus at a rate of interest which will, at the same time, give value to the currency and the funded debt, they depreciate the currency and the debt, requiring the currency to be funded at a depreciation of thirty-five per cent. for a six per cent. bond. If funded at par, as I propose, the value of the bond would regulate the value of the currency.

McCulloch, in his Dictionary, says that—

During the reigns of William and Anne, the interest stipulated for loans was very various. But in the reign of George II, a different practice was adopted. Instead of varying the interest upon the loan according to the state of the money market at the time, the interest was generally fixed at 3 or 3½ per cent, the necessary variation being made in the principal funded. Thus suppose the Government were anxious to borrow; that they preferred borrowing in a 3 per 100 stock, and that they could not negotiate a loan for less than 4½ per 100; they effected their object by giving the lender in return for every £100 advanced £150 3 per cent. stock—that is, they bound the country to pay him or his assignees £4 10s. a year in all time to come, or otherwise, to extinguish the debt by a payment of £150. In consequence of the prevalence of this practice, the principal of the debt now existing amounts to nearly two-fifths more than the sum actually advanced by the lenders.

In a note we are referred to the 93d No. of the Edinburgh *Review*, where we are told that "in 1781, a loan of £12,000,000, or $60,000,000, was negotiated, and for this sum the Government gave £18,000,000 (or $90,000,000) of 3 per cent. stock, and £3 000,000 (or $15,000,000) of 4 per cent. stock. On the whole, therefore, £660,000 (or $3 300,000) of interest was paid for this loan, being rather more than 5½ per cent; and a fictitious capital was created in favor of the lender of no less than £9,000,000 (or $45,000,000)! But it is obvious that, had this loan been negotiated without any increase of capital at 6, or even 6½, per cent, the charge on the account might have been reduced in the course of half a dozen years to 3 or 3½ per cent. on the £ 2,000,000 (or $60,000,000) actually borrowed; whereas, owing to the mode in which it was contracted, nothing could be deducted from the annual charge without being previously prepared to offer the holders £21,000,000 for the £12,000,000 (or $105,000,000 for the $60,000,000) they had originally advanced.

The *Review* adds:

Nothing, we are sorry to say, is more easy than to point out innumerable instances of this sort, in which the public interests have been sacrificed, *not intentionally, indeed, but through ignorance,* or desire to grasp at an immediate advantage in the most extraordinary manner. The very next loans negotiated by Lord North, in 1782, was for £13,500,000, for which Government gave £13,500,000 of 3 per cents; and £6,750 000 4 per cents., exclusive of an annuity of 17s. 6d. for every £100 advanced for seventy-eight years. The country was in this way bound to pay an interest of £793,125 a year, inclusive of the annuity, being at the rate of £5 16s. 10d. per cent.; and it was rendered impossible to reduce this heavy charge at any future period without previously consenting to sacrifice £6,750,000.

But it is unnecessary to go back to the American war for proof of the extreme inexpediency of funding in this manner. Most of the loans negotiated during the late (French) war were funded in the same way, and some of them on still more ruinous and improvident terms on the part of the public. Thus, according to the terms on which a loan of £18,000,000 sterling was bargained for in 1795, a capital of £21,000,000 3 per cent. stock and £4,500,000 4 per cents., exclusive of a long annuity of £58,500, were assigned to the subscribers. But the terms of the loan of £13,000,000, negotiated in 1798, were still more extravagant. For every £100 advanced entitled the lender to £175 3 per cent stock, £20 4 per cent. stock, and an annuity of 6 shillings for 62¾ years; or, in other words, for every £100 advanced to the Government, it bound the country to pay an annual interest of £6 1s, exclusive of the long annuity of 6 shillings

The *Review* then adds further:

The improvidence of this transaction is glaring and obvious. There can be no manner of doubt that an addition of from ¼ to ½ per cent. would have procured this loan without any increase of principal; but supposing that 1 per cent additional interest had been required, instead of being subjected to a constant payment in all time to come of £5 12s. 4d., for every £100 advanced, we should have had £6, or £6 10s. to pay for three or four years, and £3, or at most £3 10s. ever after.

By way of illustrating the system in a still more striking light, and bringing the results of the different operations connected with the funding of the

British national debt during the French war, into one point of view, the *Review* gives a statement of loans contracted in each year, from 1793 to 1816, both inclusive; of the amount of all sorts of stock created on account of these loans; of the total interest on dividend payable on them; of the portions of said loans paid to the commissioners of the sinking fund; of the amount of all sorts of stock purchased by said commissioners; and of the amount of the dividends on said stock.

Upon this exhibit, the *Review* remarks that—

It appears, then, that the sums borrowed on account of the public service, during the late war, really amounted to £396,352,206; and it also appears that an excess of $173,028,782 (£569,380,988—£396,352,206), of capital or stock, was created in favor of the lenders, over and above the sums advanced by them, being at the rate of nearly fifty per cent. on the sum lent. And it further appears that, the whole annual charge on account of the money borrowed during the late war, amounted, at its close, to £21,006,631 being at the rate of about 5¼ per cent.

But it is evident that had the sums thus borrowed been funded, without any artificial increase of capital, in a 5¼, a 5¾, or a 6 per cent stock, the charge on account of interest might now have been reduced from 5¼ to 3 or 3½ per cent., or from *twenty-one* to *twelve* or *fourteen* millions!

It thus appears from this statement that the British public are now paying 3 per cent. per annum, on £172,078,782, more than they would pay if the loans had been contracted at par; and McCulloch says that between 1822 and 1824, by an application of part of the surplus revenue and the reduction of interest on the 4 and 5 per cent. stocks, existing in 1817, and by that paid on the unfunded debt, the total annual saving by the reduction of interest, between 1822 and 1824, has been £2,355,845, or $11,779,225. If to this be added interest, at 3 per cent., upon the £173,028,782, or $865,143,910—the excess created by the erroneous system of funding—it will give an an annuity of $37,633,542, which compounded at 3 per cent., will, in forty-one years, give the sum of $3,089,426,392.

If the loss to the British Government and people, by their system of borrowing and funding £396,352,206 (equal to $1,961,761,392), was, in 41 years, $3,089,426,392, what will be the loss to the people and Government of the Confederate States by our present system of borrowing and funding the sums required to "carry on the Government of the Confederate States?"

Whilst I am writing, a morning paper says: "We understand, from an authority which we regard as altogether reliable, that the features of a bill for arming the negroes and placing them in the field, is being canvassed by a circle of politicians, prior to the introduction before the Confederate Congress. The bill proposes—1st. To conscribe all the able-bodied negroes of the country, between the ages of 18 and 45, respectively. 2d. To organize this force into regiments, brigades and divisions, and to arm and equip them thoroughly as soldiers. 3d. To officer the forces thus organized from meritorious soldiers and subalterns now in the field. 4th. *To offer each negro who serves faithfully to the end of the war his freedom.*"

Coupled with the suggestion that we are not fighting for the institution of slavery, this is, indeed, a most startling and alarming proposition—To arm and train our negroes as soldiers, with the promise of freedom in case they serve faithfully to the end of the war!! What would be the inevitable effect of such a measure? Would it not, of itself, accomplish all that the North can do by the most successful prosecution of the war? Would it not substitute the Northern for the Southern social organization and characteristics? Would it not be worse than reconstruction? Would it not be subjugation? Would it not deprive us of the labor requisite to produce cotton and tobacco, and thus deprive us of the means of sustaining our credit and of transferring to the consumers of British goods a large part of the burden of our public debt? Under such circumstances, I feel it to be my duty to give a brief notice of the rise and progress of Abolition in England and in the United States, and to call upon the people, and especially upon our gallant army, to unite in denouncing a measure so unwise, and to mark with the severest reprobation any public man who dares to give to it the slightest encouragement, countenance or support.

### ENGLAND AND THE SLAVE TRADE.

By the 16th article of the treaty of Utrecht, England confirmed the contract made by the English Guinea Company with the King of Spain, by which that company gave to Spain 200,000 crowns, and to the Kings of Spain and of England each one fourth part of the profits of their trade, for the privilege of supplying the Spanish American Colonies with African slaves. This was in 1713. It is well known that England compelled Virginia, regardless of her remonstrance, to receive slaves imported by the Yankees.

England, then, engaged in the slave trade because it gave employment to British ships and large profits to British trade.

In 1817, England gave to Spain two millions of dollars to abolish the slave trade!! Why, after having given Spain 200,000 crowns and one fourth part of the profits of the trade, for the privilege of supplying her colonies with slaves, did England give to Spain two millions of dollars to abolish the slave trade? Wilberforce, in his discussion of the treaty in the I onse of Commons, gave the answer. He says:

I cannot but think that the grant to Spain will be more than repaid to Great Britain in *commercial advantages*, by the opening of a great continent to British industry—an object which would be entirely defeated if the slave trade was to be carried on by the Spanish nation. Our commercial connection with Africa will much more than repay us for any pecuniary sacrifices of this kind. I myself will live to see Great Britain deriving the greatest advantages from its intercourse with Africa.

That we may the better understand the motives which govern the measures and policy of England, it is proper that we look into her domestic and colonial systems, and first, of

### THE COLONIAL POLICY OF ENGLAND.

I quote from the Edinburgh *Review*, of August, 1825:

The act of 1650, passed by the Republican Parliament, laid the foundation of the monopoly system, by confining the import and export trade of the Colonies exclusively to British or Colony built ships. But the famous Navigation Act of 1660 (12 Charles II, cap. 18) went much farther. It enacted that certain specified articles, the produce of the Colonies, and since well known in commerce as *enumerated* articles, should not be exported directly from the Colonies to any foreign country; but that they should first be sent to Britain, and there unladen (the words are, *laid upon the shore*), before they could be forwarded to their final destination. Sugar, molasses, ginger, fustic, tobacco, cotton and indigo were originally enumerated; and the list was subsequently enlarged by the addition of coffee, hides and skins, iron, corn, lumber, etc. . . . But the insatiable rapacity of monopoly was not to be satisfied with compelling the colonists to *sell* their produce exclusively in the English markets. It was next thought advisable that they should be obliged to *buy* such foreign articles as they might stand in need of, exclusively from the merchants and manufacturers of England For this purpose it was enacted, in 1663, that no commodity of the growth, production or manufacture of Europe, shall be imported into the plantations, but such as are laden and put on board in England, Wales, or Berwick-upon-Tweed, and in English built shipping, whereof the master and three fourths of the crew are English. . . . . . . It was also a leading principle in the system of Colonial policy, adopted as well by England as by the other European nations, to discourage all attempts to manufacture such articles in the Colonies as could be provided for them by the mother country. The history of our Colonial system is full of attempts of this sort; and so essential was the principle deemed to the idea of a Colony, that even Lord Chatham did not hesitate to declare in his place in Parliament, that the British Colonists in North America had *no* RIGHT *to manufacture even a nail for a horse shoe!* And when such were the enactments made by the Legislature, and such the avowed sentiments of a great Parliamentary leader and a friend to the Colonies, we need not be surprised at a declaration of a late Lord Sheffield, who did no more, indeed, than express the decided opinion of almost all the merchants and politicians of his time, when he affirmed thus: THE ONLY *use of American Colonies or West India Islands is* THE MONOPOLY *of their consumption and the carriage of their produce.* . . . . . . Were it not for the perverse and most injurious regulations to which this system has given rise, we might supply ourselves with sugar from the East Indies or South America, for a great deal less than it now costs to buy it from the West India planters. This is a much more serious loss than is generally supposed. Sugar has become a necessary, equally indispensable to the poor and the rich. The quantity of West India sugar, annually consumed in Great Britain, may, we believe, be taken on an average at about 380,000,000 of pounds weight. And it has been repeatedly shown, that a reduction of the duties on sugar from the East Indies and South America, to the same level with those laid on West India sugar, would enable us to obtain as good sugar for 4½d. per lb, as now costs 6d.; but taking the difference at only 1d. per lb, it would make on the above mentioned quantity a saving of no less than £1,583,000 ($7,915,000) a year. . . . . . Not only, however, do we exclude the sugars of the Dutch colonies, Brazil and Louisiana, but we actually lay 10s. a cwt. of higher duties on the sugar imported from our own dominions in the East Indies, than on that which is imported from the West! Not satisfied with giving the West India planters a monopoly of the home market against foreigners, we had given them a monopoly against our own subjects in the East. It is impossible to speak too strongly in condemnation of this arrangement—not that we mean to insinuate that the East Indians have any right whatever to be more favorably treated than the West Indians; but we contend that they have a clear and undoubted right to be as favorably treated. To attempt to enrich the latter, by preventing the former from bringing their produce to our market, or by loading it with higher duties, is not only to prefer the interests of *one* million, and those—we do not say it disparagingly of the planters—mostly slavers, to the interests of one hundred millions of subjects; but is totally inconsistent with, and subversive of, every principle of impartial justice and sound policy.

It is said, however, that slavery exists in Hindostan as well as in Jamaica, and that by reducing the duties on East India sugar and facilitating its cultivation, by allowing Europeans to purchase and farm lands, we should not get rid of the evils of slavery, but would be merely substituting the produce of one species of slave labor for another. Now, admitting for a moment that this statement is well founded, still it is certain, from the cheapness of free labor in Hindostan, no slaves ever have been, or ever can be, imported into that country. And hence it is obvious that, by substituting the sugars of the East for those of the West, we should neither add to the number nor deteriorate the condition of the existing slave population in our dominions, while we should save above *a million and a half* in the purchase of one of the principal necessaries of life, at the same time that we subverted a system of monopoly and laid the foundations of a new and extensive intercourse with India—a market which may be enlarged to almost any conceivable extent."

Here is the key which unlocks the motives, and controls and regulates the measures and policy of England. To encourage and foster the slave trade, she had given to the West Indies a monopoly of the supply of the home market with tropical produce—the discovery of the power loom, the cotton gin and the spinning jenny had so increased her manufactures that it had become necessary to find new markets for the sale of the surplus products of her machinery, and hence she emancipated her West India slaves, and opened the trade of India to British enterprise. The motive is indicated by historical facts as well as by her arguments. Thus, in 1825, the Edinburgh *Review* assails the West India monopoly upon the ground that its repeal would lay the "*foundation of a new and extensive intercourse with India*—A MARKET WHICH MAY BE ENLARGED TO ALMOST ANY CONCEIVABLE EXTENT."

The appeal to the pocket nerve of England, however, prevailed, and as Wilberforce urged, in 1817, that the grant of two millions of dollars to induce Spain to abolish the slave trade would be more than repaid by opening to England the commerce of the continent of Africa, which could not be done so long as Spain was permitted to carry on the slave trade, so, in 1833, it was argued that the one hundred millions of dollars paid to the West India proprietors would be more than repaid to England by the increased commerce with India, which "would be entirely defeated," unless the West India monopoly was repealed; and this could not be done without first emancipating the West India slaves and indemnifying the West India proprietors.

The prevailing impression in England then was, that free labor was cheaper than slave labor, and that the effect of opening the trade of India would be to so reduce the price of tropical products that it would be equivalent to the confiscation of the West India estates, and, therefore, the indemnity given was, in fact, a remuneration for the depreciation of West India property, caused by admitting into the British market the cheaper produce of the East Indies; and the emancipation of the West India slaves was but an act of justice to their masters in remuneration for the destruction of the value of their property, and not an act of mercy or of sympathy for the slaves.

This is proved not only by the fact admitted by the Edinburgh *Review*, as quoted above, that slavery existed then in the East Indies, and continues to exist there now, and is enforced by the authority of British law, but by the further fact that, finding that the cheap slave labor of India cannot successfully compete with the slave labor of America, the diplomatic energies of England have been exerted to increase the value of the tropical products of India by the abolition of slavery wherever slave labor elsewhere has come in competition with the labor of India. The war now waged against us is the fruit of the abolition movement of England, and to arm and emancipate our slaves would be the consummation of her efforts to aggrandise her power and influence by the destruction of that principle of our social and political organization which constitutes the basis of our strength and prosperity. It is admitted that slavery exists in India, but, who ever heard a British statesman or a British press denounce the slavery of India? Why does England send her sympathies on a voyage of discovery to Africa and America, instead of enlisting them in behalf of her own suffering poor in England, in Ireland and India?

That there may be no doubt as to the motive of England, I quote from Lord Stanley in the House of Commons in 1842. He said that on sixty-two sugar estates in the British West Indies, the loss from January to December, 1841, had been $983,000 on an outlay of $1,250,000; and Sir Robert Peel said, "He must say he had his doubts if a colony, in which slavery had been abolished by law, could at present enter into successful competition with a district in which the system continues to exist."

Urged on by these convictions, England has not only continued slavery in India, but, by a system of internal police, she has levied upon the free labor, as well as the slave labor, of India exactions much more onerous than are laid upon our slaves.

McCulloch, speaking of the revenue and expenditure of the East India Company, says: "The far greater part of the revenue of India is, at present, and has always been, derived from the soil. The land has been held by its immediate cultivators generally in small portions, with a perpetual and transferable title; but they have been under the obligation of making an annual payment to the Government of a certain portion of the produce of their farms, which might be increased or diminished at the pleasure of the sovereign, and which has, in almost all cases, been so large as seldom to leave the cultivators more than a bare subsistence. Under the Mahomidan Government, the gross produce of the soil was divided, into equal or nearly equal shares, between the ryots or cultivators, and the Government We regret we are not able to say that the British Government has made any material deduction from this enormous assessment. Its oppressiveness, more than anything else, has prevented our ascendancy in India; and the comparative tranquility and good order we have introduced from having the beneficial effects that might have been anticipated The cultivators throughout Hindostan are proverbialy poor; and, until the amount of the assessment they are at present subject to be effectually reduced, they cannot be otherwise than wretched. They are commonly obliged to borrow money to buy their seed and carry on their operations, at a high interest, on a species of mortgage over the ensuing crop. *Their only object is to get subsistence*—to be able to exist in the same obscure poverty as their forefathers. If they succeed in this they are satisfied. Mr. Colebrook, whose authority on all that relates to India is so deservedly high, mentions that the quantity of land occupied by each ryot or cultivator, in Bengal, is commonly about six acres, and rarely amounts to twenty-four; and it is obvious that the abstraction of half the produce raised on such patches can leave the occupiers nothing more than the barest subsistence for themselves and their families Indeed, Mr. Colebrook tell us that the condition of ryots, subject to this tax, is generally inferior to that of a hired laborer, who receives the miserable pittance of two annas, or about three pence a day wages. Besides the land revenue, a considerable revenue is derived in India from the monopolies of salt and opium, the sale of spirituous liquors, land and sea customs, post office, etc. Of these monopolies, the first is, in all respects, decidedly the most objectionable Few things, indeed, would do more to promote the improvement of India than the total abolition of this monopoly. An open trade in salt, with moderate duties, would, there can be no doubt be productive of the greatest advantages to the public and a large increase of revenue to the government. The opium monopoly, the less objectionable than the last, is, notwithstanding, very oppressive. It interferes with the industry of the inhabitants—*those who are engaged in the cultivation of opium being obliged to sell their produce to the Government at prices arbitrarily fixed by the Company's agents*"

Finding that the labor of India could not compete with the slave labor of America, England, in 1840, negotiated what she termed her slave trade treaty, which was intended to be an amendment to the law of nations authorizing her to arrest, on the high seas, any ship suspected of being engaged in the slave trade, to be carried into British ports and condemned by British Judges. And such was the tone of the British press, and such the character of British diplomacy, that the President (Mr. Tyler) deemed it expedient to send me as a confidential agent to London, where I spent several months writing a series of articles for the *Morning Chronicle.* From London I went to Paris, and wrote a series for the *Journal of Commerce.* The ratification of the treaty was before the French Chamber of Deputies. There was then a slaveholding interest in the French West Indies. My arguments were addressed to that interest and to the continental powers of Europe. I endeavored to unmask the purpose of England, and to show that the emancipation of American slaves would enable England to exchange her manufactures for the tropical products of India, which products she would then sell to consumers on the continent at much higher prices than would otherwise be paid to the American producers. I urged and aided General Cass, to write his protest against the ratification of the treaty. My articles were reproduced in the French Chamber of Deputies. They were translated and circulated in Germany, and the ratification of the treaty, was defeated.

Whilst in Paris I had a free and confidential conversation with one of the leading diplomatists of England (Sir Henry Ellis), to whom I urged the necessity of an early and satisfactory adjustment of the issues, then pending with the United States, as the only means of preventing a combination, between the United States and Russia, and other leading powers of Europe, for the purpose of emancipating the British East Indies, and opening the commerce of India to all the world. He urged me to write out the substance of my remarks for him, saying that he wished to send them to Lord Aberdeen. I found it impossible to prepare a communication sufficiently respectful to be submitted to His Lordship, and, instead, wrote an article giving extracts from the official reports of the poor law commissioners, proving the condition of the laboring poor of Ireland and England to be much more degraded than that of our slaves, and charging that the purpose of England was to substitute the tropical products of India for those of America, and that having by her experiment in the West Indies ascertained that the cheap labor of India could not successfully compete with the slave labor of America, her efforts to abolish the slave trade and to emancipate African slaves were prompted by the hope that if, under the pretence of sympathy for the slave, she could accomplish this, then she could obtain tropical produce from the East Indies in exchange for her manufactures, and thus levy tribute on the consumers of East India produce at the same time, that by the monopoly of the trade to India she could greatly increase her manufactures, her shipping and her navy. That such is her purpose, I proceed to quote authorities which place the matter beyond question:

### THE DUKE OF WELLINGTON.

In the debate on the Corn Laws in 1842, the Duke of Wellington said:
I am sure no man laments more than I do that commerce of manufactures should be at all depressed; but I believe if the Corn Laws were repealed to-morrow, not a yard of cloth or a pound of iron more would be sold in any part of Europe or of the world, *over which this country does not exercise a control.* My Lords, the greatest number of European nations, and of the nations of the globe, have adopted measures for the encouragement of home manufactures. These measures were not, as stated by some, taken in consequence of the English Corn Laws. They are attributable to the example of this

ntry. They had their rise in the spectacle which this country exhibited during the s war, and in the great and noble exertions by which her power and strength were played on every occasion. Those who contemplated these exertions, as well as those o were relieved and assisted by them, thought they might as well follow the example our power, of our industry, and our system of commerce. They have followed our imple, and have established among themselves manufactures, and given a stimulus their commerce.

### LORD PALMERSTON.

In the debate on the state of the country, on the 6th July, 1842, Lord ilmerston having explained that the markets of France and Germany were )sed to British manufactures, said :

I therefore look to more distant regions for future prosperity. We must look to the ing nation which inhabits the North American continent. There we are met by our orn Laws, and until we alter these we will be crippled in our commercial intercourse re must look also to South America. There again we are met by heavy duties on gar, and until these are modified we cannot expect to carry on commerce with South merica to the extent it is possible. We must look again to Africa, and we must look pecially to India and to China.

### MR. COBDEN.

That the *animus* which governs the measures and policy of England may better understood, I quote from a pamphlet written in 1835 by Mr. Cob en. He says :

We are on the eve of a novel combination of commercial necessities that will al gether change the relation in which we have hitherto stood with our colonies. We ll them necessities; they will be forced on us, not from our conviction of the wisdom such change, but by the irresistible march of events. The new world is destined to ;come the arbiter of the commercial policy of the old. * * *. It is to the indus y, the economy and peaceful policy of America, and not to the growth of Russia, tha it statesmen and politicians, of whatever creed, ought to direct their most anxious udy; for it is by these and not by the efforts of barbarian force that the power and reatness of England are in danger of being superceded; yes, by the successful rivalr f America shall we in all probability be placed second in the rank of nations. * *

Bearing in mind that the supply of the raw material of nearly one half of our ex orts is derived from a country that threatens to eclipse us by its rival greatness, w annot, whilst viewing the relative position of England and the United States at thi ioment, refrain from recurring to the somewhat parallel cases of Holland and Grea ritain before the latter became a manufacturing State.

* * *. The latter (England) now sees in America a competitor in every respec alculated to contend with advantage for the sceptre of naval and commercial supre nacy.

### FRAZER'S MAGAZINE RECOMMENDS SERVILE WAR.

In 1841 Frazer's *Magazine* published an article headed " War with Americ blessing to mankind," in which, after laboring to enforce the propriety of eclaration of war by England, and the necessity of making a war subserv nt to the great and permanent object of freeing our slaves, he says : " Polic ot less than philanthropy prescribes such a course of warfare," and add:

In one morning a force of ten thousand men could be raised in Jamaica for the e ranchisement of their brethren in America. Such a force, supported by two battalio f Englishmen and 20,000 muskets, would establish themselves in Carolina, never to l emoved. In three weeks from their appearance, the entire South would be in one co lagration. The chains of a million of men would be broken, and by what power cou hey ever again be rivetted? We say that this course is dictated alike by self-preserv ion and by philanthropy.

It will thus be seen that the programme of the invasion of Virginia l

John Brown, and the Federal scheme of a servile war, originated in England. Even now, Earl Russell and Mr. Lindsay both declare that if England could be satisfied that the purpose of the Federal Government is to emancipate our slaves then the sympathy of England would be with the North. And why does England wish to emancipate our slaves? It is because she believes that then the cost of producing cotton, rice and sugar in America would be so much increased that her cheap labor in India could drive the American cotton, sugar and rice out of the market.

### SIR ROBERT PEEL.

The debate in 1842 on the proposition to repeal the tax on Cuban and Brazilian sugar, Sir Robert Peel said:

To open our markets to the sugars of Cuba and Brazil would detract from the high character this country (England) has acquired in its efforts and sacrifices to put down the slave trade. * * * What I say is, make the attempt—try to get concessions from those of whom we get our supply—those countries themselves are in a peculiar position. You may depend upon it that there is a growing conviction among the people of those countries that slavery is not unaccompanied with great dangers. In Cuba, Brazil, and in the United States, there is a ferment on the subject of slavery which is spreading and will spread. Some from humane and benevolent motives—some on account of interested fears, begin to look at the great example we have set, and begin to look at the consequences which may result from that example nearer home.

This speech was made in opposition to a proposition to repeal the duty on Cuban and Brazilian sugar, based upon a petition which alleged that the tax on these sugars was $47,085,715 per annum. The argument, interpreted, was "pay this tax a little longer and I will soon be able to induce Cuba and Brazil to abolish slavery, and then the United States will follow their example," for, said he in addition: "It is impossible to look to the discussion in the United States, and especially to the conflicts between the Southern and the Northern States without seeing that slavery in that nation stands on a precarious footing." And why should Sir Robert Peel urge the people of England to continue to pay a tax of $47,085,715 per annum, under the hope that it would aid in the emancipation of our slaves? In the same debate he said:

I must say that I have my doubts if a colony in which slavery has been abolished by law can, at present, enter into competition with a district in which the system continues to exist.

And Lord Stanley, then a member of the Government, said that, on sixty-two West India sugar estates, from the 1st of January to December, 1841, the actual loss to the proprietors was $983,000 on an outlay of 1,269,000 dollars. These extracts prove that

### THE CHEAP LABOR OF INDIA CANNOT COMPETE WITH SLAVE LABOR.

The Government and people of England have become satisfied that cheap as the labor of India is, it cannot successfully compete with the slave labor of America, and they therefore wish to emancipate our slaves, believing that, if to this be done then they can compel the people of India to exchange the raw products of India for British manufactures, upon terms that will increase the power, wealth and resources of England.

In proof of this I quote further from Sir Robert Peel. He said:
The honorable member for Montrose announced his wish to maintain our colonial de-

ndencies, but said that his object was to see each colony paying for itself. I apprehend that the proposal of the honorable and learned member from Bath to admit an limited competition with slaves possessing colonies is not the way to insure that object. The honorable member said that if the weavers of Lancashire were asked what benefit they derive from the duty on foreign sugar, they will assuredly say—"none." It I put it to the honorable member whether that is the test by which any great question affecting this country is to be decided? If I ask a Lancashire weaver what benefit he derives from Jamaica, and his reply is—"none," ought that to induce me to abandon my measure? Is the honorable gentleman prepared to test the advantages derived from our connexion with India in the same manner? or should we abandon our colonial dependencies altogether, upon the assurance of a distressed weaver of Lancashire, that he is not aware that any benefit is conferred upon this country by our dependencies? If that be the principle of the honorable gentleman, it is quite clear that it in order to conform to it we must resolve ourselves into the narrow limits of our own resources and try what England can do against the world, after having abandoned all those dependencies which she has established to her glory.

Yes, England, under pretence of benevolence, would pay a tax of forty-seven millions of dollars, under a hope that, by the emancipation of our slaves, she could drive us out of the market, and then she would bind the poor East Indians to the muzzle of her cannon, and shoot them into fragments, by way of compelling India to exchange her raw products for British manufactures, because she hopes, by such means, to monopolize the greater part of the trade in tropical produce and thus increase her power and resources. Is it not obvious that for this she repealed the duties favoring West India produce, emancipated the West India slaves, and opened the trade of India to British subjects? Is it surprising that she refuses to recognize the Confederate States?

### BRITISH POOR LAWS.

Before the act of 1833, any English laborer, whose wages were not sufficient to maintain him and his family, was entitled to receive such an allowance from the poor rates as would make the sum requisite for their support. This was termed "out door relief," and could be claimed only by those who were *settled* in the parish. To obtain a settlement required that an applicant should have been born in the parish, or have been in service twelve months, or the owner of a freehold worth ten pounds per annum.

The Edinburgh *Review* for May, 1828, quotes a member of the House of Commons, who said:

This forced and expensive way of relieving the poor has put many gentlemen and parishes upon contriving all possible methods of lessening their number, particularly by discouraging, and sometimes hindering, poor persons from marrying, when they appear likely to become chargeable, and thereby preventing an increase of useful laborers, by discharging servants in their last quarter, and preventing them from getting a settlement, whereby they become vagrants—by pulling down cottages and suffering no places of inhabitation for paupers, whereby estates are flung into a few hands, and several parishes are, in a measure, depopulated. England complains of a want of useful hands for agriculture, manufactures, for the land and sea service; and, for remedying this, a bill for a general naturalization was lately introduced. * * * But no scheme, I believe, will ever succeed so long as parishes are so apprehensive of paupers, and take all manner of precaution to prevent a multiplication of inhabitants.

Again, from Arthur Young:

There is no parish but had much rather that its young laborers would continue single; in that state they are not in danger of becoming chargeable; but when married the case alters. All obstructions are, therefore, thrown in the way of their marrying; and none more immediately, than that of rendering it as difficult, as possible for the men, when married, to procure a house to live in; and *this conduct is found so conducive to easing the rates, that it universally gives rise to an open war against cottages.* . . . . The Act of 43d Elizabeth, by devolving the protection of the poor on the landlords and occupiers of land, compelled the latter to take all possible precautions to prevent the too rapid increase of the former., A premium was given to those who lived in a state of celibacy; early and improvident marriages were discouraged by what could not fail to be considered very severe penalties.

The *Review* adds:

The able-bodied tenant of a workhouse should be made to feel that his situation is decidedly less comfortable than that of the industrious laborer who supports himself, *and that a life of unremitting toil, supported on coarse and scanty fare, is to be his portion* so long as he continues in this degraded state.

It adds further:

Dr. Burn, who is one of the very highest authorities as to all that respects the poor, has given the following graphical delineation of the peculiar business of a parish overseer: The office of an overseer of the poor seems to be understood to be this: To keep an extraordinary lookout, to prevent persons coming to inhabit without certificates, and to fly to the Justices to remove them; and if a man brings a certificate, then to caution the inhabitants not to let him a farm of £10 a year, and to take care to keep him out of all parish offices. To warn them, if they will hire servants, to hire them by the month, the week, or the day, rather than by any way that can give them a settlement; or, if they do hire them for a year, then to endeavor to pick a quarrel with them before the year's end, and so to get rid of them; to maintain their poor as cheaply as they possibly can, and not to lay out two pence in prospect of any future good, but only to serve the present necessity; to bargain with some sturdy person to take them by the lump, who is not yet intended to take them, but to hang over them *in terrorem,* if they shall complain to the justice for want of maintenance; to send them out into the country a begging; to bind out poor children apprentices, no matter to whom or to what trade, but to take special care that the master live in another parish; to move heaven and earth, if any dispute happens about a settlement; and, in that particular, to invert the general rule and stick at no expense; *to pull down cottages; to drive out as many inhabitants, and admit as few, as they possibly can—that is, to depopulate the parish in order to lessen the poor rate;* to be generous indeed sometimes in giving a portion with the mother of a bastard child to the reputed father, on condition that he will marry her; or with a poor widow, always provided that the husband be settled elsewhere; or, if a poor man, with a large family, happen to be industrious, they will charitably assist him in taking a farm *in some neighboring parish,* and give him £10 to pay his first year's rent with, that they may thus for ever get rid of him and his progeny.

The *Review* quotes the *Morning Chronicle* as saying:

These restraints which persons of property, *interested in putting down poor rates,* will infallibly impose, are much more likely efficacious than those he (the laborer) will impose on himself. Until lately, no pauper could marry, *and no pauper ought to be allowed to marry.* If there was no opening for a married man in his own parish, and if the attempt to marry in another led to his removal as a pauper, the laborer found himself governed by circumstances to which his inclinations were forced to yield.

So much for the Edinburgh *Review.*

The London *Quarterly,* of December, 1832, says:

1st. The able-bodied laborer must be discouraged from relying on parish aid. 2d. He must be enabled to maintain himself in independence. The first end is to be attained only by requiring from all parish laborers *full work for a rate of pay barely sufficient to support the individuals.* A mere subsistence, in return for their utmost exertions, is all that, in justice or policy, the parish can or ought to be compelled to afford them. Harshly as this may sound, it is absolutely necessary, to prevent our degenerating into a nation of paupers, that *the parish should always have the character of the hardest task-masters, and the worst pay-master a laborer can apply to.*

It will be seen that the system is so organized as to compel the able-bodied laborer to work, and to reduce the compensation below the point of subsistence. The *Review* gives the following as the pay allowed to infirm poor in a county in the west of England per week:

| | |
|---|---|
| To every adult pauper, | 3s. 0d |
| Infirm paupers under 18 and above 10 years of age, | 2s. 0d |
| Children under 10 years of age, | 1s. 3d |

PAY OF PARISH LABORERS PER WEEK.

| | |
|---|---|
| Single man, | 3s. 0d |
| Man with a wife, | 5s. 0d |
| Young men and women under 18 and above 12 years, | 2s. 0d |
| Single women, | 2s. 6d |
| For each child incapable of work, | 1s. 3d |
| Boys and girls under 12 years of age, | 1s. 6d |

The Edinburgh *Review* says that it has been "affirmed, and truly, that there was no considerable increase of population in England from the period when the poor laws were first established (1601) up to the middle of the last century; and it is alleged that its recent increase has been wholly owing to the prodigious extension of manufactures and commerce;" and the London *Quarterly*, of March, 1826, says:

We are inclined to suspect that in all agricultural districts the population suffered a diminution by no means inconsiderable during this interval (from 1550 to 1750). For the purpose of investigating this point, we have consulted a variety of parish registers, considering these as the most certain sources of authentic *data* for forming an opinion on the subject. The register book of the parish in which we are now writing commences about 1550. On an average of fifty years, the number of baptisms annually entered in it stands thus:

From 1550 to 1600, 50 per annum.
From 1600 to 1650, 53 per annum.
From 1650 to 1700, 34 per annum.
From 1700 to 1750, 19 per annum.
From 1750 to 1800, 19 per annum.
From 1800 to 1824, 34 per annum.

There is nothing peculiar either in the situation or circumstances of this parish. It is situated in a country purely agricultural, near one of the main public roads, and at no great distance from the Metropolis. The land is divided into farms of very moderate dimensions, and a considerable portion of it is copyhold, a circumstance forming, at all times, a powerful impediment to the demolition of houses of husbandry and the consolidation of farms.

The laboring poor, under the regulation of the wages of labor, in England, have not increased in these agricultural districts for more than two hundred years; whilst, under our system of slave labor, the four hundred thousand African slaves brought to this country by the Yankees have increased to more than four millions in less than one hundred years. Could there be a stronger or more satisfactory test of the two systems?

## APPENDIX A.

It will be seen by what I have written, that I am enabled to trace the Abolition movement of the North to the purpose of organizing the *North* as a sectional political party, upon the basis of emancipating our slaves, digested by Mr. Adams, as far back as 1815, in concert with British Abolitionists. I refer to this fact now, and to the efforts which I have heretofore made to arouse the people of the slaveholding States to the necessity of counteracting the Northern sectional organization, and that up to the election of Mr. Lincoln, I did not despair of preserving the Union by restraining the action of the Federal Government within the limits of the powers granted by the Federal Constitution. In proof of this, I refer to the explanation which I have given of the Nullification of South Carolina, to which I would add an appeal which I made to the people of the slaveholding States, in 1850, given in this appendix below. I would refer now to the fact that the Federal Government was organized by the States as States, and that that Government has no powers but those granted by the Constitution, and that the question of slavery was expressly reserved to the States. The purpose of the North is dominion, power. If it were possible for them to subjugate the South, then, instead of independent, or co-equal States, we will be subjugated colonies, and the fate of Ireland, and of India, and of the pauper population of England, should admonish us of what our condition will then be.

The following address was published in 1850. It will be seen that it contemplated the possibility of preserving the Union. He who desires a reconstruction must be deaf to all the teachings of history.

### TO THE PEOPLE OF THE SLAVEHOLDING STATES.

The Jews were a peculiar people, chosen of God, and under His guidance and protection, until, as a punishment for their sins, He permitted Samuel to anoint Saul to be their King. As in His goodness and mercy, under the Mosaic dispensation, God committed the Ark of the Covenant to their keeping, so has He, in like manner, committed to the slaveholding race of this favored country, the maintenance and preservation of our Republican institutions. How is this to be done? God requires that man should labor. Idleness is sinful, and will surely be punished. Neither health, strength, power, intelligence, wealth, or influence, can be preserved without labor. We must, therefore, meet the issues involved in the present crisis, investigate their origin and progress, and prepare with a united energy for the defence of our rights and interests.

We are told that what was written aforetime was "written for our learning, that we, through patience and comfort of the Scriptures might have hope." Christ Himself said, "Search the Scriptures, for in them ye think ye have eternal life, and they are they which testify of me." He wrought miracles because it was part of His divine mission to convince his immediate disciples and the world, that He was the Son of God, having power to save sinners; but He Himself appealed to the Prophets, because their words, verified by their fulfillment in subsequent ages, are so many living witnesses, appealing to the judgments and consciences of men, confirming the truth of Revelation. Indeed, the prophecies concerning the destruction of Jerusalem—the character, dispersion, persecution, and preservation of the Jews—the desolation to befall Judea, Ammon, Moab, Idumea, Philistia, Ninevah, Babylon and Tyre, testify unto us, who live in this enlightened age, that the Scriptures are true, with even greater force than the miracles wrought in the presence of His immediate followers by our Saviour himself; for our knowledge of those miracles depends upon the testimony of those who bore witness of them, whereas the literal fulfilment of the prophecies are constantly proclaiming, in language which no one can deny, that the Scriptures are true. We then turn to the Scriptures and find that God said unto Adam, "Because thou hast hearkened unto the voice of thy wife, and hast eaten of the tree of which I commanded thee, saying, thou shalt not eat of it; cursed is the ground for thy sake, in sorrow shalt thou eat of it all the days of thy life; thorns and thistles shall it bring forth to thee, and thou shalt eat of the herb of the field; in the sweat of thy face shalt thou eat bread, until thou return unto the ground, for out of it thou wast taken; for dust thou art and unto dust shalt thou return."

We thus see that God's decree is, that man must labor, and that no one is exempt therefrom. He, therefore, who complains that the African is made to work, arraigns the wisdom, goodness, and justice of God himself. Are we told that the complaint is not that the African is made to work, but that he is a slave? We find that the first prophecy after the flood was by Noah, in these words: "Cursed be Canaan, a servant of servants shall he be unto his brethren. Blessed be the Lord God of Shem, and Canaan shall be his servant. God shall enlarge Japheth, and he shall dwell in the tents of Shem, and Canaan shall be his servant."

God is not controlled by accidents. He has a wise and beneficent purpose in all that He does. He made the earth, the fowls of the air, the beasts of the field, the fish of the sea, and the man "to have dominion over them." He made the climates and the seasons, and intended that each should act its part in the great purpose of creation. He made the lands within the tropics produce, in great abundance, articles indispensable to the comfort and happiness of man. He gave to the descendants of Ham a physical organization and constitution which enable them to endure the exposure and fatigue, without which, the rich lands of that climate cannot be brought under "the dominion of man;" and yet, although no one who believes the Scriptures can deny that the purpose of God was, that man should subdue the earth, all must admit, that, without the aid, the guidance, and control of the Christian white man, who, for want of a like physical organization and constitution, cannot labor under a tropical sun, the savage African, endowed as he is, and otherwise qualified for the task, never would put the fairest and most productive part of the habitable globe under cultivation. And the fact that the most powerful combination ever witnessed in the civilized world, acting in the name of religion and humanity, cannot suppress the slave trade, should admonish us that God has a purpose to accomplish through African slavery. And who can now doubt what that purpose is? Look upon Africa, and what do we see? A vast continent teeming with an idolatrous population, unable to subdue the earth, or otherwise fulfill the great end of their creation. God works by means that He may accomplish His purpose. What has He done through African slavery? Has he not brought millions of benighted savages to dwell under the droppings of His sanctuary? Has He not given them the blessings of the Gospel, and greatly improved the condition, physical, temporal and spiritual, of the savage African? Compare His way with the ways of man. He arrests the savage in the midst of superstitious idolatry, and, by force, places him under the protection of Christian laws, and within the influence of the Christian religion, and has thus brought millions to a knowledge of the truth. Now, how doth man work? Where are the fruits of his labor? Where are the African souls whom he hath saved? How many heathen have those who denounce African slavery converted to God? Verily, by their works will they be judged.

Who that looks over the habitable globe, and reflects upon the purposes of God, as indicated by the wants, necessities, habits, condition and history of men, can believe that the lands within the tropics are to be occupied by savages, beasts of prey and venomous reptiles? And who that is not misled by a false philanthropy, can believe that these lands can ever be brought under man's dominion, so as to contribute their due share to man's comfort and happiness, in any otherwise than that by the labor of Africans, regulated and directed by the intelligence and perseverance of white men?

It will thus be seen that African slavery was intended by an all-wise Providence to promote our happiness and prosperity; and that He had this end in view when He placed the black race under the control of the greater intelligence of the white, and made it the duty and interest of the Christian master to protect, educate, civilize and Christianize the slave. This institution has been assailed—a combination more powerful than any other formed upon earth is arrayed against it, and we alone are left to defend it.

The press and the pulpit are the great elements of modern power. We are assailed through the press and the pulpit, and through the press and the pulpit we must be defended; we must convince our own judgments and relieve our own consciences, that we may unite in support of African slavery as a *permanent* institution. We have no alternative. *We must protect our rights as masters, or we become worse than slaves.* We must go into our own mountains; we must educate our own daughters; we must qualify them to become governesses and teachers, that they may educate our children, and themselves become the mothers of sons worthy to inherit and qualified to defend our property and our institutions. We must encourage our own merchants; we must employ our own mechanics, lawyers, doctors, teachers, professors, and ministers of the Gospel; and, above all, we must employ our own editors. We must make railroads, connecting our seaports with the great West, and open a direct trade with Europe. We must revise our monetary system, so as to employ our own capital in maintaining our own credit, instead of handing over the products of our industry to the agents of foreign bankers, subject to the fluctuations of the foreign market, which those bankers can regulate at pleasure. We must print our own books, and especially our own school books. We must create a Southern sentiment, and unite our own people. We must educate our sons to command our armies, and prepare to maintain our rights, peaceably, if we can, forcibly, if we must.

That the South may act in concert and with efficiency, a Southern Education Society has been organized and chartered by the State of Georgia. The charter and the constitution of the Society are hereto annexed. The Legislature have also incorporated a female college and a university, to be located at Dalton, in this State. They have also incorporated a city company, who, as the proprietors of the city property, have agreed to give twenty thousand dollars from the proceeds of the sale of lots, if a like sum is contributed by other persons. The Society will send agents throughout all the Southern States, for the purpose of soliciting contributions to its funds, and as soon as a sufficient sum is obtained, they will commence the publication of books, and put their schools into operation.

They have issued the prospectus of the *Southern Statesman*, and, as the paper will be the property of the Society, and the profits derived from it applied in aid of the Female College, it is hoped that the entire Southern public, and especially the ministers of the Gospel and the ladies of the South, will exert themselves to obtain subscriptions and donations to place the publication on a permanent and efficient basis. The prospectus explains its purpose and objects.

It will be seen that the managers of this Society must be Baptists, and that the University and College will be under their control. We are prepared for objections. It has been said, and will be again repeated, that such institutions should not be under sectarian influence. We place these institutions under Baptist control, because, while we invite the co-operation and solicit the aid of persons belonging to all other religious denominations, and also of those who are not members of any church, we rely chiefly upon members of the Baptist society for the means of building them up and giving them efficiency; hoping that our success, as pioneers in a field which requires so many laborers, will stimulate other churches to follow our example. It will further be seen that the Society wish to educate Baptist missionaries, who shall go from our schools into the non-slaveholding States for the purpose of establishing Baptist churches in those States in fellowship and communion with the Baptist churches in the Southern States, and thus bring the combined influence of religion and patriotism in aid of the Federal Union, and that this proceeding must necessarily be of a denominational character. In further vindication, we add, that other Christian churches have established sectarian schools and colleges, and that it will be fortunate for them and for the country if our example should induce them to be more careful in the selection of teachers.

We are aware that, as our newspaper will treat of political subjects, it will be said that our purpose is to blend religion and politics. The greatest of temporal blessings is a good government. We admit that Christ's kingdom is not of this world, but we, as men, have our relations to temporal as well as spiritual matters; and it is no less the duty of Christian men to resist Satan's influence in affairs of State than to resist it in the government of the Church.

* P. S.—It may be well to add a few words in further illustration of the plans and purposes of the Southern Education Society.

No one, who will carefully read the history of the past, can doubt that the infidelity which preceded the French Revolution led to the massacres which marked that period, nor can any one who carefully examines the Scriptures fail to see that the false philanthropy and the false religion which have arrayed the Abolitionists of the North against the peace and perpetuity of this Union, is the legitimate offspring of that false philosophy which, in the name of reason and humanity, deluged the world in blood.

It is the purpose of the Southern Education Society, through its publication, to examine into the history of the past, to employ able writers to prepare a series of school books and other publications suited to the times in which we live, and free from the morbid and sickly sentiment which is the peculiar characteristic of most of the books now in use.

An estimate has been made, showing that the profits on the Northern books and publications used in the South, would feed, clothe, and educate several thousand females. The Southern planters must necessarily occupy large tracts of land, and are compelled to send their children from home or employ private teachers. John Q. Adams was one of the most active Abolitionists. It was under his advice that Daniel P. Cook moved the Missouri restriction in Congress, and under his advice Governor Slade, of Vermont, organized an Education Society, who are sending into the South and West hundreds of Abolition Missioners, in the shape of beautiful women, who, trained for the purpose, go in search of husbands, and, as teachers and governesses, are introduced into our families, train up our daughters, and marry our sons, thus building up in our midst a morbid feeling on the subject of slavery, which saps the foundation of our prosperity. It was thus that Adam was driven from Paradise.

We must counteract these proceedings by educating our own daughters to be teachers and governesses; and this we can do if the people of the South will unite in aid of the efforts of this Society.

THE FOLLOWING IS THE CONSTITUTION OF "THE SOUTHERN EDUCATION SOCIETY."

*Whereas*, The Baptist churches in the non-slaveholding States, heretofore in fellowship and communion with the Baptist churches in the slaveholding States, have instituted new rules of faith and practice, which deny to slaveholders their equal rights of conscience and equal religious privileges, and which rules of faith and practice have a direct tendency to create sectional prejudices, operating upon the religious and political opinions of the people of the non-slaveholding States; in such manner as to endanger the peace and harmony of the people of the United States, and by inducing strife and animosities, greatly to prejudice the cause of civil and religious liberty, which all men should promote by all proper means; therefore, the undersigned, having this end in view, do hereby organize themselves into a Society, to be called "The Southern Education Society," and do ordain and establish for its basis and government the following Constitution:

ARTICLE 1. The objects of this Society shall be to promote the cause of Education generally, and especially in all the slaveholding States—to qualify females to become teachers in common schools, in public and private academies, and in private families, and also to qualify all who in the Southern States are, to exercise an influence over public opinion, and especially the rising generation, the graduates of our colleges, and all men who are hereafter to fill public stations, whether in the pulpit, at the bar, or in the Legislature or in Congress, to assert, vindicate, and maintain all the rights which belong to us as citizens of the United States, and especially,

1st. Our rights of conscience and equal religious privileges;
2d. Our rights as citizens and equal political privileges;
3d. Our right to hold slaves as property; and that it is illegal and a gross violation of propriety and of good faith, for the people of any non-slaveholding State of this Union, and especially for the Legislature of any such State to do any act whatever, which may in any wise diminish the value of our slaves, or endanger, or disturb our peaceful enjoyment of such property.

ARTICLE 2. The means by which this Society proposes to act, are:
1st. The endowment and support of Female Seminaries, in which females may be qualified to become teachers in public and private schools, and in private families, and thus economize the cost of education, by bringing into requisition the character, talents and influence of woman, and permitting her to do her part in aid of the great cause of civil and religious liberty.

2d. The endowment and support of Common Schools and Colleges, in which the teachers and professors shall be persons whose opinions on these fundamental questions are known and approved.

3d. To create a literature for the South, by the publication in the South, of school books, bibles, hymn books, periodicals and newspapers, and, as far as practicable, all other books and publications suited to or required by the public; and, with this view, to establish Bible Societies, Sunday School Societies, Tract Societies, and Auxiliary Education Societies, auxiliary to the Southern Education Society:

4th. To qualify Ministers of the Gospel, who, holding the Constitution of the United States in one hand and the Holy Bible in the other, shall go forth from our Colleges as missionaries to the non-slaveholding States, rebuking the sinful proceedings in those States, and especially the Pharisaical pretensions to greater holiness; teaching their churches Christian charity and brotherly love, and planting churches in those States, wherever two or more can be found who will stand forth as witnesses of the truth, and willing to become members of a church in fellowship and union with the churches of the South.

## APPENDIX B.

The following are extracts from the article referred to on page 60, which I published in London:

OF THE UNITED STATES; THEIR FORM OF GOVERNMENT, AND THEIR RELATION TO SLAVERY AND THE SLAVE TRADE.

In explaining their relation which the United States bear to the subject of slavery, we must look to the organization, the powers, and purposes of the Federal Government. The United States were originally colonies, settled under the authority and subject to the crown of Great Britain. One of the grievances of which they complained before the Revolution, was, that the mother-country compelled them to receive African slaves, imported by authority of British law.

The immediate cause of the Revolution was, the attempt of the British parliament to tax the colonies. This led them to scrutinize the principle of taxation. They saw that no representation in parliament would protect them against oppression; that the right of taxation was in fact a right of conversion, and that to permit parliament to levy taxes, was to surrender their property to the destruction of that body. This principle was carried into the struggle of the Revolution. The colonies dispersed over so large an extent of territory, saw clearly that their Congress, composed as it was of delegates representing different sectional interests, would sympathize with the interests which they represented, and that they, too, might abuse the power of taxation. Hence the Congress of the Revolution had no power to levy taxes. They were but an advisory council. Men and money were furnished by the States. Each State was a distinct and separate independent government. Each State had a distinct organization; its governor, its legislature, its judiciary, its civil and military officers. Upon declaring themselves independent of the mother-country, each State organized their respective governments for themselves. The people of slave holding States were compelled to take into consideration the state of their society as it then existed.

The question was not whether they would institute slavery; it had already been instituted by the British Government. The black man was already the property of the white, by the law of England.

Is it matter of surprise that, under such circumstances, the master believed that his slave was not qualified by habits, education, or intelligence, to exercise political rights?—that the black man was not the equal with the white, and that legislation could not make him so?—that to emancipate the slave, without giving him equal political rights, would have created a degraded *caste*, which, so far from contributing to their moral or physical improvement, would have led to their still further degradation? and that, to have given them equal political rights, constituting them a part of the Government itself, would have inoculated the Government with a moral disease, which must have caused its premature decay? Is it surprising that they should have believed that the public safety forbade to engraft the blacks upon the body-politic, and that they had no alternative but to recognize and continue the pre-existing system of slavery? Having resolved to do this, they passed laws to ameliorate the condition of the slave, and placed him under their protection. They identified the interest of the master and the slave, and compelled the master to provide him sufficient food and raiment. Instead of living on dry potatoes, as is the case with the Irish laborer, the American slave has an abundance of wholesome diet, and to spare. Instead of sleeping upon wet straw, with a single poverty blanket for a whole family, as in Ireland, the American slave has good bedding and an abundance to spare of bed-clothes. Instead of one suit in seven years, as in Ireland, he has his three new suits—one for winter and two for summer, and good shoes and stockings. Instead of killing them by unmitigated toil long before they become burthensome, through age or infirmity, as charged by the Edinburgh *Review;* and instead of permitting them to perish by exposure to hunger and cold, as in Ireland, the American slave is nursed in sickness, and comfortably provided for in his old age.

We have said that the colonies, in declaring themselves independent, refused to organize a Central Government with the power of taxation; that the Congress of the Revolution was but an advisory council, and that the States were separate sovereignties. As such, on the 4th of July 1776 they declared themselves independent, which independence, as separate sovereign States, was recognized by England herself in the treaty of peace.

These separate sovereign States thus became a part of the society of nations, who recognised their right to establish their own form of Government, and, in doing so, recognised the institution of slavery as by them established. After they had thus been admitted into the family of nations—after their forms of Government, including the institution of slavery, had been recognized and adopted, they determined to form a more perfect union, and for this purpose the States selected delegates, who met in convention and proposed for their adoption the present Federal Constitution. In that convention each State had the same voice, and the constitution thus prepared had no binding force until it was adopted by nine States, and then only as between the States so adopting it. It will thus be seen that the Federal Constitution is a compact between sovereign and independent States.

These States carried into the convention great diversity of opinion. Some of the delegates were in favor of a monarchy; some preferred a President and Senate for life; many desired to create a strong Central Government; but the conflict between the colonies and the mother country had begotten a repugnance to monarchy; and an apprehension that a strong Central Government would end in the despotism of an absolute majority, in which the interest of the weaker sections would be sacrificed by combinations of the stronger, induced the weaker States to insist upon reserving an equal voice in the Senate, and to resist every attempt to give the Federal Government any further domestic control than was indispensable to union among themselves, and to a successful administration of their foreign relations. The Federal Constitution, therefore, while it constitutes them one distinct nation as to all the rest of the world, is but a compact between sovereign States, regulating their intercourse with each other, which compact was not intended to interfere with the Constitution or form of Government pre existing in the several States, who, in adopting it, considered and treated each other as separate Governments.

Slavery had been *established* by Great Britain, and *continued* by the States in which it had been thus established, because the people of those States, in declaring themselves independent of the mother country, did not believe that they could, consistently with their own safety, or the happiness of the blacks themselves, change the relation which the British Government had forced upon them; and the other American States, in forming the Federal Constitution, had no more right to insist that the slaveholding States should abolish slavery, and to make that a condition of their becoming parties to the Federal Government, than France or England had to require it as a condition to the treaty of peace, by which their independence was established. In fact, the question of slavery never has been submitted to the American people as such. The question before them was not whether slavery should be abolished, but whether they should become parties to the Federal Constitution. In doing so, the several States became members of the Federal Government, reserving to themselves the exclusive control over their domestic institutions. And hence, as domestic slavery was a domestic institution, and under the exclusive jurisdiction of the respective States, the Federal Government being charged with the foreign relations of all the States, is alike bound to protect the interest and property of all; and hence, so long as any State shall recognize the property of the master in his slave, the Federal Government is as much bound to protect that right of property as it is to protect the right of property of the merchant in his ships. This brings us to the case of the *Creole*, where slaves, the property of an American citizen, on board an American ship, passing from one American port to another, prompted by assurances that if they could reach a British port, they would be liberated, rose upon the crew, murdered part of them, and compelled the others to navigate the ship to Nassau (New Providence), where they were set at liberty by the British authorities. The case cannot be strengthened by argument. The Federal Government was constituted to protect the rights of property of the slaveholder in all questions arising between him and foreign Governments. We know that very high authority have declared that there is no law in England which will authorize the delivery of these slaves. We hold that slaves, by the law of nations, are admitted to be property; that while on board an American ship, they are slaves; and that a vessel carried by mutiny into a neutral port is not subject to the municipal regulations of that port; and that the seizure of these slaves was an illegal confiscation.

Can any one suppose that the American Government would permit any other Government to confiscate an American ship carried into a neutral port under such circumstances? And if they would not permit the confiscation of the ship, how can they, without dishonor, permit the confiscation of the slaves?

They are as much bound to protect the property of the Southern planter as of the Northern merchant.

Thus, in the working of this complex system, the institution of slavery counteracts the influence of universal suffrage, and prevents the ascendancy of that absolute majority, of the evils of which M. De Toqueville was apprehensive; and, therefore, the American statesman places a much higher estimate upon it than the mere right of property; and the intelligent European will see that it constitutes a distinct element in American society, acting upon the machinery of government, which is not applicable to the States of Europe.

The London *Times* tells us that "the British Government has, with great exertions, managed to conclude treaties, by which the slave trade is to be punished as piracy; that the right of searching American ships is indispensable to its execution, and that the British Government is determined to enforce it." Following upon the heels of this, even before these treaties are ratified, we have an order in council authorizing the transportation of East India emigrants to the island of Mauritius, and we are told that extensive arrangements have been made to transport emigrants from Africa to Jamaica, Trinidad and Guiana. The 20th article of this order in council, which bears date January 14th, 1842, is in the following words: "No emigrant, arriving from India at Mauritius, shall, in Mauritius, be capable of entering into any contract for service except for the period, in the manner, and under the superintendence, which, by a law in force there, is required in case of contracts for service by other laborers in agriculture or manufactures within the said island."

This order provides for the emigration of free labor, and requires that such laborer shall be incapable of making a contract, except by a law made by the party giving him employment. Now hear what the Edinburgh *Review* says in relation to free labor in Jamaica, and the means used by the law-makers in Jamaica, to reduce the price of free labor below that of slave labor. "It has been attempted," says the *Review* "to make the dwelling and provision-ground of the negroes the instrument of compelling them to work for the land-holder, on whose plantation they reside, or reducing their wages!" The language used has been, if you do not work for me, you must immediately quit your house and land (to the latter of which its tenant has given its principle value); if you demand so much a week for wages, I demand so much a week for rent, or rather so much for each member of your family, without reference to the actual value of the tenement and its appurtenances, and the one demand and the other shall be simultaneously adjusted; the strong arm of the law has been liberally invoked to carry on the contest commenced on such grounds; in some instances the administrators of the laws, enactments of the most heterogeneous description have been brought to bear upon the unfortunate laborers; there are the contract act, the poundage act, the fishery act, the huxter act and pedlar act, the police act, and the vagrant acts.

When we come hereafter to speak of the suffering poor of Ireland, the reader will understand the process by which free labor is reduced below the cost of slave labor. But here again we recur to the Edinburgh *Review*. It says: "When slavery is tempered with ordinary humanity, what Mr. Gurney calls the 'dead weight,' the maintenance of the old, the infirm, the sick. the shammers of sickness, the mothers of young infants, and the numerous children, make the aggregate expense ruinous."

Such is the theory of British philanthropy; and, therefore, in order "to beat Cuba and Brazil out of the market," they substitute free labor for slave labor, and leave the old, the infirm, the sick, the widow and orphan, to perish of hunger and nakedness! But this is not enough. The same *Review* tells us "that the proposition for declaring the slave trade piracy, assumes that the right of search and seizure should be exercised, and that the culprit should be prosecuted in the courts of this (Great Britain), and not of the culprit's, country."

But hear the *Reviewer*. He says: "The poverty of India must be cured by the attraction of British capital to the fields of production. United as it happily is with England, it NEVER can become a manufacturing country, * * * * * being happily disabled, by their relative position, from levying contributions upon each other, by domestic industry-protecting tariffs, the people of India may employ themselves profitably for a period, to which it is impossible to fix a limit, in raising raw produce to exchange for the manufactures of Great Britain. Both the capital and the intelligence necessary even for this purpose must come from England."

But it may be well also to look to the comparative resources of the two countries. America has no debt; she has all the materials of war within herself. She has men, provisions, arms, and all the munitions of war; and all these she can command *at home,* by means of her power of taxation and her credit. *She will not be compelled to come to Europe for a dollar.* She has the material for navies, also, and these she can produce and equip with the facility of magic. She has six hundred steamboats on a single river, and these can be converted into a fleet, bearing men and provisions, that will drive the piratical fleets of England and the West Indies. But would she be content with this? Would she not declare the emancipation of the British colonies? Would not France, and Russia, and Holland, unite with America in breaking the chains which bind down the independence of Ireland and of India? Instead of compelling all the world to come to purchase India cotton, and India sugar, will not all the world unite with America in declaring the servitude of Ireland and India to be at an end? And would not this be accomplished? Is this the just retribution which an all-wise Providence has decreed as the punishment for the sins of England? and is the struggle of the British land-owner, to maintain his position in society, to end in this? What, then, is to become of British power? Who, then, will pay British rents and British taxes?

We will not attempt to probe the subject further. If Great Britain would avoid the consequences, she must retrace her steps; if, indeed, the day of retribution has arrived, she will persevere.

## APPENDIX C.

The traditionary policy of Russia, from the time of Catherine, has been to seize upon Constantinople as the gate to the commerce of India; and hence England, jealous of the progress of Russia, has sustained the power and dominion of the Turk against the encroachment of Russia. Preliminary to a renewal of the war with the Sultan, Russia created a large fleet at Sebastopol. As a means of perpetuating his dynasty, and hoping to secure the co-operation of England, Napoleon the Third became a party to the war in the Crimea, and not only destroyed the Russian fleet, and not only prevented a control of the Black sea, but closed the Dardanelles to Russia. Shut out from the commerce of India by way of the more direct route, the emissaries of Russia were soon found in the north of China and the Japanese seas, and proposals were issued for a loan to be applied to the construction of a railroad from St. Petersburg on the north of China, to the mouth of the Amoor river. Seeing that such a railroad would, unless otherwise prevented, give to Russia a preponderating influence in China, and endanger the British supremacy in India, England induced France to unite with her in the war upon China, by which the monopoly of the trade of China by Russia was prevented. With this introduction, I give in the appendix an article from the London *Spectator*, of April 11, 1857, which, as was intended, defeated the Russian loan, and has delayed, for how long remains to be seen, the construction of the contemplated railway.

The power thus described by the *Spectator* acts in concert, and lives and moves, and had its being, in the delusion that nothing but gold or silver is money. Its profits depend upon its control over the exchanges, which are regulated by the movement of money and of commodities.

### THE NEW POWER IN EUROPE.
[*From the London Spectator, April* 11, 1857.]

The present state of affairs on the Continent suggests the existence of some influence which is not generally recognized, though its power must be overruling and its operation universal. It is not seen, yet it reverses the councils of governments which appear to be supreme; it disregards equally public opinion and the interests of the States in which it has its agents. The monetary condition of France and of Northern Europe draws attention once more to the irregular and dangerous speculation which the most powerful man in Europe tries in vain to curb; it would seem that there is some greater power than he, irresponsible and absolute; and when we turn to ascertain the fact, we are not long in discovering at least enough to create uneasiness and to demand scrutiny. We perceive some corroborative proof that such an influence does exist—that its power is becoming supreme—that it is now doing mischief, and that it may become dangerous alike to the material condition, the political independence, and the domestic order of

States. Nor are we speaking of any imaginary or mere "moral" influence; we speak of a powerful combination more than political, more personal than a Congress of diplomatists or princes.

The Emperor Napoleon has long been engaged in the endeavor to draw out the enterprise of his subjects, and the effect throughout France is great. Any traveller in the most outlying provinces perceives a remarkable change in the aspect, action, and condition of the people. The trading class, as well as the industrial classes, are animated by a spirit of energy hitherto unknown to the Celtic population. They have learned not only to employ their time with more vigor, but employ their savings—to venture that which they once hoarded. In that economical sense France was almost a virgin soil, and the effect is described by the traveller as marvellous. Thus far a blessed change. But look beyond. The very capitalists who fostered if they did not implant the idea in the Imperial mind, have seized the same opportunity to project movements for the further development of capital, its power and productivity. The great speculator in this sense differs in some degree from the ordinary trader. The money merchant obtains his profit entirely from the simple act of exchange, and he does so equally whether the original holders are profiting in the transaction or not. He may be the broker between two communities who are ruining each other, and build his fortunes upon their downfall. And the individual trader in this merchandise will be instigated principally by the desire to grasp large and prompt profits. He is not a safe councilor for those who have in charge the permanent interests of States. For the welfare of a community, immensely accumulated wealth, hoards of gold, are not so essential as well diffused supplies of the necessaries of life and its enjoyments. But the same movement which gave an impulse to the commercial spirit in France made the largest opening that the world has ever seen for a forward movement of great capitalists; and they have snatched it. Alarmed at the vast proportions which these joint-stock combinations have attained in France, the Emperor and his political ministers have issued their protest against excesses in that direction; they have followed up protests with restrictive imposts; but still the movement goes on

The commercial activity directed to the development of real trade would, with as much steadiness as rapidity, increase the available means of the French people—would make them more independent of the casualties of the seasons—would make them more comfortable, more orderly, more capable of supporting their ruler, more obedient to his decrees. It is easily to be understood why the Emperor Napoleon desires to add that element of English order to the military capabilities and energy of the French. He has in great part succeeded. But the excess of speculation invoked by those who have stood ready to take advantage of the impulse has, again in the present moment as it did in the autumn of last year, threatened to defeat the improvement by over-doing it; and we in England are under the same commercial pressure which visited us in the autumn. At the same time there appears to be no suspense in developing, extending and multiplying the immense joint stock combinations which the French Emperor has endeavored to restrain, though at such a time such operations ought to be entirely suspended. We see on the stocks the new International Society of Commercial Credit, whose founders are connected with the great money corporations in every capital of Europe—the banks of France, England, Amsterdam, etc. The list of the Council of Administration of the grand company lies before us. Of the great Russian Railway Company, half of the members short of one are Russians, and the great number in that half are Councillors of State and officers in the service of the Emperor Alexander. In that Russian half, however, we see the name of " Thomas Baring, banker, in London." The other half consists of men whose names are well known in every capital: S. Gwyer, member of the Council of Commerce; Earnest Sillem, a partner in the house of Hope & Co., at Amsterdam; Guillaume Borski, banker in Amsterdam; Francis Baring, banker in London; Henri Hottinguer, banker in Paris; Isaac Pereire, administrator of the Paris and Lyons Railway; Baron Seillere, banker in Paris; M. Auguste Thurneyssen, administrator of the West of France Railway; and M. Louis Fould, brother of the well-known State financier. Some of those are the names we so constantly encounter in that comparatively small list of men who are administering the greatest financial operations in Paris, Vienna, St. Petersburg, Amsterdam and London. The object of this company is to take forty-five millions of capital, a sum which could easily be raised for reproductive purposes, but which they intend to sink in railways through the Russian deserts; while the actual state of the whole world—of Europe, England, America, and the far East—proves that we cannot spare that forty-five millions, nor even the first instalment of it Yet these few gentlemen, who rule the world at present, have determined that it shall be taken, despite the Emperor of the French, the Bank of England, or the commercial public of this country.

It is said that the position of M. de Morny is not satisfactory either to the Emperor of all the Russias or to the Emperor of the French; but M. de Morny is fulfilling a career which has become independent of Emperors. He has attached himself to the Grand Council of the International Finance, and it is that Grand Council at present which arranges the affairs of the world by the power of the purse, let potentates and parliaments think what they may. The Emperor of the French is at present engaged in attempting to restrain the use of fictitious titles—counties, vis-counties and baronies—baubles at which the aristocracy of wealth may laugh. The power of that order, which is the more powerful because its members are comparatively limited, proceeds in its actions independently of those ordinary political movements, and shows itself pursuing its course uninterrupted, undiverted, whatever may be the state of the commercial world, whatever may be the mood of the Imperial mind, whatever may be the action of ordinary statesmen.

We are not considering the diversion of capital, the dangers that may arise from over speculations, the ruin that may visit shareholders in these huge joint stock companies, from which the directors always withdraw before the crash. We are not considering the commercial disturbance created by the necessity, which is forced upon Europe just at present, of undergoing a high rate of interest for ordinary commercial accommodation, while millions are lavished upon the fancies or the schemes of those millionaire statesmen. We are simply considering the magnitude and the independence of that power of combined millions. It is a new order—a new administration in the world. The names most conspicuous in it are remarkable for certain characteristics. Read them again—Rothschild, Baring, Steiglitz, Pereire, Hottinguer and Fould; with a second order, comprising the Weguelihs, the Hopes, and the Seillieres. They form a grand council of small numbers that could all be assembled in a dining room. They are remarkable for being closely connected with the Governments of all the principal States in the world, while, at the same time, they are not closely connected with the States under those Governments. You would not accept a Baring as being peculiarly representative of England; you must choose many other names before it—the Russels, the Stanleys, the Salts, the Crawshays, Cobdens and Tyrells. France would certainly not be represented by Pereire, no country by a Rothschild; a Steiglitz is by no means exclusively Russian, any more than Fould is French. The class is alien to any particular country, and yet is deeply rooted in the administration of each country. It can command not only a mass of capital enough to determine the financial operations of a Government, the success or failure of a State loan, but it can influence, beneficially or fatally, the course of trade, by turning upon any one branch the combined mass of capitals from States elsewhere, just as the five potentates of Europe can muster an army which would crush the people of any one empire mutinying against any one of the five. But this grand council of millionaires has proved that it is superior to the political administration of the separate countries. It is at once alien to the aristocracy of any country, and yet becoming more powerful, and therefore more respected, than any one aristocracy. Unlike any order which we have yet seen, it has its home equally in Paris, Berlin, Vienna, Amsterdam, St. Petersburg or London. It is republican, but of the aristocratic republic, more close than the Grand Council of Venice, infinitely more arbitrary. Like that commercial republic, kings bow down to it; but the kings that now bend are the giant emperors of our day, not the brawling leaders of the middle ages. The debates of this council are not reported; its constitution is as yet unascertained and undetermined. We feel its power before we can define it. It is independent of political councils, higher than political responsibilities, ignorant of constitutional checks. It stands confessed in the actual events of the present week; and in its independence, perhaps disregard of the interests which it overrides, it extorts from us the question whether any account has yet been taken of the immense institution that has sprung up while Emperors and common politicians were thinking to settle the world with armies and treaties.

The aggregation of capital and credit and financial influence, thus described, was the fruit of the system of funding and finance adopted by the British Government acting through the Bank of England, and represents the profits created by dealing the public credit of European and other Governments, and which, having concentrated into so small a circle so great a control over public credit, from time to time so acts upon the commerce and exchanges of the commercial world as to regulate the value of money and of property, regardless of pecuniary losses which they inflict on those who may be the victims of their remorseless speculations. Thus, as I have stated:

### AMERICAN CREDIT IN ENGLAND.

Prior to 1838, any American merchant, who could obtain an acceptance of either Wilde, Wiggins or Wilsons, three American houses established in London in connection with the American trade, could purchase British goods upon a credit of six and twelve months, and as our commercial system was then organized, he could, by giving his Custom House bond, get time to pay the duties. "He was thus enabled, by the use of his credit, to command British capital in the shape of merchandise, and having made sales, he could with the proceeds purchase American produce, which, being remitted to the credit of the London House, was sold, providing funds to meet his payments.

### THE FINANCIAL SYSTEM OF ENGLAND HOSTILE TO THE CONFEDERATE STATES.

Corresponding to the emancipation of the West India slaves, and the opening of the East India trade, the capitalists and financiers of England opened a bitter and relentless warfare on American credit, which resulted in the prostration of American credit in England, and a new organization of the American trade; under which, instead of their giving us their capital upon our credit, we gave them our capital upon their credit. The *modus operandi* was thus: An agent of a British banker or manufacturer bought cotton or other exports in a Southern port, and made payment in a bill payable sixty or ninety days after date, in New York, which bill was discounted by our banks, because nor merchants, no longer able to buy goods in Manchester, bought them in New York, and therefore, funds in New York were worth more than funds in the Southern banks. The bill upon New York, when due, was paid by a second bill upon London, which was discounted by the banks of New York, because the New York merchants dealt in Europe, and money in London was worth more than money in New York. When this second bill became due, the cotton had reached Liverpool and had been sold to the manufacturer, whose note at ninety days had been discounted, and the proceeds placed to the credit, not of the Southern planter or of the Southern merchant, but of the British agent, who was thus enabled to fix the price in our market, and of course took into consideration all the cost and charges, and the contingencies affecting the price in Liverpool, and especially the fact that he would be compelled to sell the cotton in Liverpool in time to meet the payment on the second bill. Consequently the price thus fixed was the lowest at which the combination of English cotton spinners (the cotton supply association acting in concert with their agents), could purchase in our market. The merchants and the banks of New York were also deeply interested in this new system, because it made New York the port of entry for the South, and gave to New York merchants and New York banks the profits which have built their marble palaces, and multiplied their wealth and resources.

The effect of this re-organization of the American trade was to reduce the price of cotton from *seventeen* cents to three, and the effect of reinstating the control of this "new power" in Europe over the values of the money, the property, and the credit of this county, by resuming specie payments, will be to reduce us to a condition equally, or even more, oppressive than the Egyptian bondage of the Israelites.

DUFF GREEN.